General editor: Graham Handley MA PH D

Brodie's Notes on William Shakespeare's

The Merchant of Venice

W. Baker M Phil PH D
Senior Lecturer in English, West Midlands College

Pan Books London, Sydney and Auckland

First published 1985 by Pan Books Ltd
Cavaye Place, London SW10 9PG
19
© copyright Pan Books Ltd 1985
ISBN 0 330 50187 9
Photoset by Parker Typesetting Service, Leicester
Printed and bound in Great Britain by
Richard Clay Ltd, Bungay, Suffolk

Other titles by W. Baker in the Brodie's Notes series:
Antony and Cleopatra

Contents

References in these Notes are to the
Arden Shakespeare: *Merchant of Venice*,
but the Notes may be used with
any edition of the play.

Preface

This student revision aid is based on the principle that in any close examination of Shakespeare's plays 'the text's the thing'. Seeing a performance, or listening to a tape or record of a performance, is essential and is in itself a valuable and stimulating experience in understanding and appreciation. However, a real evaluation of Shakespeare's greatness, of his universality and of the nature of his literary and dramatic art, can only be achieved by constant application to the texts of the plays themselves. These revised editions of Brodie's Notes are intended to supplement that process through detailed critical commentary.

The first aim of each book is to fix the whole play in the reader's mind by providing a concise summary of the plot, relating it back, where appropriate, to its source or sources. Subsequently the book provides a summary of each scene, followed by *critical comments*. These may convey its importance in the dramatic structure of the play, creation of atmosphere, indication of character development, significance of figurative language etc, and they will also explain or paraphrase difficult words or phrases and identify meaningful references. At the end of each act revision questions are set to test the student's specific and broad understanding and appreciation of the play.

An extended critical commentary follows this scene by scene analysis. This embraces such major elements as characterization, imagery, the use of blank verse and prose, soliloquies and other aspects of the play which the editor considers need close attention. The paramount aim is to send the reader back to the text. The book concludes with a series of revision questions which require a detailed knowledge of the play; the first of these has notes by the editor of what *might* be included in a written answer. The intention is to stimulate and to guide; the whole emphasis of this commentary is to encourage the student's *involvement* in the play, to develop disciplined critical responses and thus promote personal enrichment through the imaginative experience of our greatest writer.

Graham Handley

Shakespeare and the Elizabethan playhouse

William Shakespeare was born in Stratford-upon-Avon in 1564, and there are reasons to suppose that he came from a relatively prosperous family. He was probably educated at Stratford Grammar School and, at the age of eighteen, married Anne Hathaway, who was twenty-six. They had three children, a girl born shortly after their marriage, followed by twins in 1585 (the boy died in 1596). It seems likely that Shakespeare left for London shortly after a company of visiting players had visited Stratford in 1585, for 1592 – according to the jealous testimony of one of his fellow-writers Robert Greene – he was certainly making his way both as actor and dramatist. The theatres were closed because of the plague in 1593; when they reopened Shakespeare worked with the Lord Chamberlain's men, later the King's men, and became a shareholder in each of the two theatres with which he was most closely associated, the Globe and the Blackfriars. He later purchased New Place, a considerable property in his home town of Stratford, to which he retired in 1611; there he entertained his great contemporary Ben Jonson (1572–1637) and the poet Michael Drayton (1563–1631). An astute businessman, Shakespeare lived comfortably in the town until his death in 1616.

This is a very brief outline of the life of our greatest writer, for little more can be said of him with certainty, though the plays – and poems – are living witness to the wisdom, humanity and many-faceted nature of the man. He was both popular and successful as a dramatist, perhaps less so as an actor. He probably began work as a dramatist in the late 1580s, by collaborating with other playwrights and adapting old plays, and by 1598 Francis Meres was paying tribute to his excellence in both comedy and tragedy. His first original play was probably *Love's Labour's Lost* (1590) and while the theatres were closed during the plague he wrote his narrative poems *Venus and Adonis* (1593) and *The Rape of Lucrece* (1594). The sonnets were almost certainly written in the 1590s though not published until 1609; the first 126 are addressed to a young man who was his friend and patron, while the rest are concerned with the 'dark lady'.

The dating of Shakespeare's plays has exercised scholars ever since the publication of the First Folio (1623), which listed them as comedies, histories and tragedies. It seems more important to look at them chronologically as far as possible, in order to trace Shakespeare's considerable development as a dramatist. The first period, say to the middle of the 1590s, included such plays as *Love's Labour's Lost*, *The Comedy of Errors*, *Richard III*, *The Taming of the Shrew*, *Romeo and Juliet* and *Richard II*. These early plays embrace the categories listed in the First Folio, so that Shakespeare the craftsman is evident in his capacity for variety of subject and treatment. The next phase includes *A Midsummer's Night's Dream*, *The Merchant of Venice*, *Henry IV Parts 1 and 2*, *Henry V* and *Much Ado About Nothing*, as well as *Julius Caesar*, *As You Like It* and *Twelfth Night*. These are followed, in the early years of the century, by his great tragic period: *Hamlet*, *Othello*, *King Lear* and *Macbeth*, with *Antony and Cleopatra* and *Coriolanus* belonging to 1607–09. The final phase embraces the romances (1610–13), *Cymbeline*, *The Tempest* and *The Winter's Tale* and the historical play *Henry VIII*.

Each of these revision aids will place the individual text under examination in the chronology of the remarkable dramatic output that spanned twenty years from the early 1590s to about 1613. The practical theatre for which Shakespeare wrote and acted derived from the inn courtyards in which performances had taken place, the few playhouses in his day being modelled on their structure. They were circular or hexagonal in shape, allowing the balconies and boxes around the walls full view of the stage. This large stage, which had no scenery, jutted out into the pit, the most extensive part of the theatre, where the poorer people – the 'groundlings' – stood. There was no roof (though the Blackfriars, used from 1608 onwards, was an indoor theatre) and thus bad weather meant no performance. Certain plays were acted at court, and these private performances normally marked some special occasion. Costumes, often rich ones, were used, and music was a common feature, with musicians on or under the stage; this sometimes had additional features, for example a trapdoor to facilitate the entry of a ghost. Women were barred by law from appearing on stage, and all female parts were played by boy actors; this undoubtedly explains the

many instances in Shakespeare where a woman has to conceal her identity by disguising herself as a man, e.g. Rosalind in *As You Like It*, Viola in *Twelfth Night*.

Shakespeare and his contemporaries often adapted their plays from sources in history and literature, extending an incident or a myth or creating a dramatic narrative from known facts. They were always aware of their own audiences, and frequently included topical references, sometimes of a satirical flavour, which would appeal to – and be understood by – the ground-lings as well as their wealthier patrons who occupied the boxes. Shakespeare obviously learned much from his fellow dramatists and actors, being on good terms with many of them. Ben Jonson paid generous tribute to him in the lines prefaced to the First Folio of Shakespeare's plays:

Thou art a monument without a tomb,
And art alive still, while thy book doth live
And we have wits to read, and praise to give.

Among his contemporaries were Thomas Kyd (1558–94) and Christopher Marlowe (1564–93). Kyd wrote *The Spanish Tragedy*, the revenge motif here foreshadowing the much more sophisticated treatment evident in *Hamlet*, while Marlowe evolved the 'mighty line' of blank verse, a combination of natural speech and elevated poetry. The quality and variety of Shakespeare's blank verse owes something to the innovatory brilliance of Marlowe but carries the stamp of individuality, richness of association, technical virtuosity and, above all, the genius of imaginative power.

The texts of Shakespeare's plays are still rich sources for scholars, and the editors of these revision aids have used the Arden editions of Shakespeare, which are regarded as pre-eminent for their scholarly approach. They are strongly recommended for advanced students, but other editions, like The New Penguin Shakespeare, The New Swan, The Signet are all good annotated editions currently available. A reading list of selected reliable works on the play being studied is provided at the end of each commentary and students are advised to turn to these as their interest in the play deepens.

Literary terms used in these notes

Irony The difference between what is said and what is actually the case. There are various kinds of irony at work in the play. The forms used most commonly are (a) **verbal irony** where a speaker says one thing and implies another. For example at the end of the first scene Antonio tells Bassanio 'my credit . . . shall be rack'd even to the uttermost/To furnish thee to Belmont to fair Portia.' The use of 'credit', 'racked' and 'fair' are ironic. On the one hand they refer to financial credit being fully stretched so that Bassanio can court the beautiful Portia. On the other hand they refer to Antonio's state of mind which will be further tortured by Bassanio's courtship of the wealthy Portia. (b) **dramatic irony** 'involves a situation in a play . . . in which the audience shares with the author knowledge of which a character is ignorant' (Abrams, *Glossary of Literary Terms*). An obvious example occurs in Act II, Scene 2. Young Launcelot Gobbo, in order to trick his father, pretends to be blind. We the audience share with the young Gobbo the knowledge that his eyesight is fine.

An example of verbal and dramatic irony working together may be found in the trial scene. Bassanio is prepared to give up 'life itself, my wife, and all the world' in order to save his friend. Portia, his wife, disguised as Balthazar, replies 'Your wife would give you little thanks for that/If she were by to hear you make the offer.' We as audience know she is 'by to hear' her husband 'make the offer.'

A third kind of irony at work in *The Merchant of Venice* is (c) **irony of action**. The most obvious example and explanation of this may be found in the trial scene when, enthusiastically, Shylock lets Portia 'look upon the bond'. Shylock's action causes his defeat.

Simile A comparison between dissimilar things indicated by 'like', 'as' or 'than' or by a verb such as 'appears' or 'seems'. Salerio in the first scene tells Antonio 'your argosies with portly sail/Like signiors and rich burghers on the flood', where the simile lies in the comparison between Antonio's ships and distinguished citizens.

Metaphor A comparison between dissimilar things without using a connective such as 'like' or 'as'. Salerio tells Antonio that his 'mind is tossing on the ocean' (Act I, Scene 1). The metaphor lies in the comparison between the mind and a ship at sea.

Pun A play on words that sound or are spelt the same but have very different meanings. This device is used throughout the play and students should see the textual notes on 'fair', 'credit' and 'rings' – to choose but three examples from the many puns in the play. See also the section on *Prose and Poetry.*

Imagery Metaphors and similes. See *Imagery* pp.87–8.

The play
Plot and plot structure, sources and date
Plot

A noble Venetian Bassanio has frittered away his fortune. In order to attempt to win the hand of the rich Belmont heiress Portia he needs to borrow money and turns for help to his rich but sad friend Antonio. Although Antonio's resources are tied up at sea, he takes out a loan in order to assist his friend. At Belmont, Portia assesses her situation with her maid and confidant Nerissa. Portia's future is determined by a chance choice. Under the terms of her father's will whoever chooses the correct casket from a choice of three wins her and her estates. If the suitor chooses incorrectly, he must leave Belmont immediately. Portia is besieged by suitors, none of whom she favours.

Antonio is forced to borrow three thousand ducats from Shylock, a Jewish money-lender. Antonio and Shylock personally dislike each other; however, Shylock agrees to lend the money not for interest but instead draws up a special agreement – a bond. If Antonio cannot repay his debt within three months Shylock will remove exactly a pound in weight from Antonio's flesh. Antonio, confident that his dispersed ships and goods will safely return to Venice within the time allotted, agrees in spite of his friend Bassanio's protests.

Back at Belmont Portia faces her suitors, who include a pompous Moroccan prince, and later a vain Aragonese prince. In Venice Bassanio prepares for his journey to Belmont. Launcelot Gobbo leaves Shylock's service bidding a tearful farewell to Jessica, Shylock's daughter, who is planning to elope with the gentile Lorenzo. Preparations are under way for Bassanio's going-away party. Lorenzo prepares to receive Jessica, who will leave her father's house with valuables. Jessica, dressed as a page, will act as Lorenzo's torch-bearer at the revels. Launcelot acts as a go-between, delivering messages between Jessica and Lorenzo. Prior to going to Bassanio's for supper, Shylock secures his house and possessions, leaving Jessica responsible for them. She elopes, and Bassanio leaves for Belmont.

As the news breaks that Antonio's ships have run aground,

Bassanio wins Portia, Gratiano declares his love for Nerissa, and Jessica arrives with Lorenzo in Belmont. These last two announce that Shylock is insisting upon repayment of his bond. Portia agrees to settle the debt and suggests that immediately after their marriage, Bassanio returns to Venice to settle the matter. In Venice Antonio has been imprisoned. An enraged, angry Shylock turns a deaf ear to pleas for mercy and demands his bond. Bassanio and Gratiano depart for Venice and Portia sets in motion her plan to assist Antonio. Lorenzo and Jessica are left in charge of the estate, whilst Portia pretends to encloister herself and Nerissa, 'to live in prayer and contemplation', until their betrothed return. In reality she is to go to Venice disguised as a young lawyer, with Nerissa disguised too as her clerk.

In the justly acclaimed trial scene Shylock demands his bond. The judge, the Duke of Venice, is just about to pronounce sentence in Shylock's favour when Portia, disguised as a lawyer, arrives with Nerissa and the tables are turned. She gives Shylock the chance to accept Bassanio's offer but he rejects this. Shylock is then defeated, for he must take the exact weight of flesh – no more and no less – and must not under Venetian law shed blood. Further, the punishment for a foreigner taking Venetian life is death, and for one seeking a Venetian life, half the property goes to the state, the other half to his victim. The Duke of Venice spares Shylock's life. Antonio proposes a settlement upon Jessica and Lorenzo of Shylock's estate, and that he administer the other half until Shylock's death, when the money will go to them. Antonio also insists that Shylock be converted to Christianity. Overwhelmed and shocked, Shylock agrees and leaves.

Portia and Nerissa return to Belmont and on the arrival of their husbands Bassanio and Gratiano, accuse them of unfaithfulness. Portia and Nerissa had, when disguised at the end of the trial scene, taken payment by insisting upon possessing the rings which Bassanio and Gratiano were to wear as symbols of their undying love and constancy. Portia then reveals the truth about her disguise and their Venetian activities. Antonio hears that his ships have been saved and Lorenzo and Jessica learn of their inheritance. The play concludes on a bawdy jesting note.

Plot structure

There are two main plots and two sub-plots. The two main plots are:

1 The bond story involving Shylock and Antonio.
2 The casket choice revolving around Portia and her suitors.

The two plots are closely intertwined because:

(a) Bassanio needs money in order to court Portia – to participate in the casket choice.

(b) In order to obtain the necessary provisions to go to Belmont he places his friend Antonio in debt. Antonio in order to please Bassanio whom he loves enters into a bond with Shylock whom he hates.

(c) Portia disguised as a male lawyer defeats Shylock.

(d) The caskets themselves point to the moral that appearances are deceptive. Bassanio chooses lead and gains Portia. Shylock chooses revenge, gains nothing, and is destroyed by Portia in disguise.

The two sub-plots are:

1 The Lorenzo-Jessica plot centering around Jessica's elopement.
2 The ring plot involving Portia and Nerissa (in disguise) and Bassanio and Gratiano. Also involved is Antonio, who urges Bassanio to give the young 'lawyer' the ring.

Both are inter-related with each other and the main plot since:

(a) Jessica's elopement with Lorenzo and her removal of valuables from her father's house fans the flames of Shylock's lust for revenge.

(b) Jessica's elopement unites, links, or 'rings' different Venetian communities – the Jewish and Christian.

(c) The rings given by Bassanio and Gratiano to Portia and Nerissa when they are disguised pinpoint the themes in the play of deception, disguise and loyalty.

(d) The rings represent wealth (rings cost money!) and emotional value – remember that the loss of his wife's ring causes Shylock enormous distress. This relationship between financial and emotional value reverberates throughout *The Merchant of Venice*.

Sources

The bond story, the pound of flesh tale, is found in ancient religious and folk tales set in Persia and India and in various different forms in Western literatures. In other words it is not a new tale but an archetype – i.e. a story which transcends cultures and religions to have a universal meaning relating to revenge and its consequences. There has been some speculation that a lost Elizabethan play, possibly called *The Jew*, and focussing upon usury existed. The casket story is also an ancient archetype. It is found, for instance, in an early 9th century Greek romance, in Boccaccio's *Decameron*, and a group of stories called *Gesta Romanorum* (a collection of medieval folk tales).

Both stories may be found in a tale called *Il Pecorone* written around 1378 by Ser Giovanni, printed in Italian in 1558. *Il Pecorone* contains the bare bones of the story to which Shakespeare's greatness adds meat. There is a young Venetian merchant who borrows money from a Jewish money-lender. The young Venetian also wishes to win the 'lady of Belmonte'. The money-lender demands the repayment of his bond through the removal of flesh. The 'lady of Belmonte' also arrives in Venice disguised as a lawyer. There is a trial, rings are exchanged, the Jew is defeated.

Marlowe's *The Jew of Malta*, first performed around 1589, focusses attention upon a villainous Jew named Barabas and his daughter Abigail, who is converted to Christianity. Barabas is presented as the embodiment of revenge and villainy – indeed as a monstrosity. Such a portrait would have fanned the flames of anti-Jewish hostility present in audiences of Shakespeare's time.

Literary anti-semitism, the figure of the evil stage-Jew reflects the history of Jewish settlement in England. Traditionally the Jew was associated with money-lending and the crime of usury: the medieval Catholic Church forbade Christians to lend money for profit. In 1290 about sixteen thousand Jews were expelled from England. There was no official return until Cromwell's invitation to Jews to re-settle in England in the 1650s. However, evidence of Jewish settlement in the late 16th century is found for instance in the Lopez trial of 1594. Dr Lopez, Elizabeth I's physician, was executed on a trumped-up charge of high treason. Marlowe's *The Jew of Malta*, although performed earlier than the Lopez case, reveals an interest in Jews and Jewish activities, and there can be little doubt that Shakespeare too in *The Merchant of Venice* was drawing upon the interest shown in the Lopez case.

Date of *The Merchant of Venice*

It is probable that *The Merchant of Venice* was written between 1594 and 1598 when it was first acted. The play was published in 1600 with the title 'The most excellent / Historie of the Merchant / of Venice / with the extreme crueltie of Shylocke the Jewe / towards the sayd Merchant, in cutting a just pound / of his flesh and the obtayning of Portia / by the choyse of three / chests.' This edition is known as the Quarto (i.e. the first separately published edition of the play). *The Merchant of Venice* appeared in the first Folio (i.e. the first collected edition of Shakespeare's Works) published in 1623.

Scene summaries, critical comment, textual notes and revision questions

Act I Scene 1

Antonio's depression is a subject of concern. Salerio and Solanio speculate that either Antonio is in love or worried about the fate of his cargoes. Antonio scoffs at these suggestions. Gratiano, arriving with Lorenzo and Bassanio, believes that Antonio is pretending to be sad in order to appear wise. Left alone with his friend, Bassanio tells Antonio that he has fallen in love with a highly sought after Belmont heiress and needs money in order to court her. Antonio's sadness is still unexplained but the strength of his affection for Bassanio is shown. He is unable directly to assist Bassanio for his 'fortunes are at sea' but will take on his behalf a loan.

Commentary

The central plots of *The Merchant of Venice* evolve from this first scene:
(a) Antonio's feelings for Bassanio will place him in debt to Shylock;
(b) Bassanio's love for Portia leads him to the casket choice;
(c) Lorenzo's reminder to Bassanio where to meet him (Act II, Scene 4) hints at his planned elopement with Jessica.

Other major elements are introduced. All the characters in Venice depend upon trade and the sea. Images of the sea, ships, fortune, wealth, gold, romance, credit, security and insecurity (financial and psychological) are found here. Evident also are the themes of friendship (Antonio's friends try to cheer him up), fidelity (his friends stay by him); pretence (Antonio finds it difficult to play a part, to act, to hide his true feelings), display (of wealth and goods) and show (to appear happy). Word-play is seen in the punning, for instance, on the words 'fair', 'good', 'worth', and 'dear'.

In sooth In truth (he doesn't know why he is so sad). The play appears to open with a reply to a question which has just been asked.

I am to learn I have yet to learn: or, will find out (as the play unfolds). Various reasons have been given for Antonio's depression: (a) worry about his goods and ships; (b) anxiety over Bassanio's friendship and the possible loss of it; (c) a general state of malaise distinguishing him from his friends. Dramatically his uncertainty creates a sense of mystery for the audience.

such a want-wit So lacking in intelligence.

much ado to know myself Unlike his previous self, unable to understand why he is in the state that he is in.

tossing on the ocean His thoughts are restless – his wealth is bobbing up and down in ocean ships.

argosies Ships loaded with luxury goods.

portly sail Expensive sailing equipment.

signiors Gentlemen of high rank.

burghers Wealthy people.

pageants . . . reverence So rich and well-equipped are Antonio's ships that they dwarf all other shipping. 'Pageants' refers also to portable structures used for plays, the forerunners of today's carnival floats.

cur'sy to them The smaller ships appear to be curtsying in deference to the larger ones.

woven wings Poetic language for 'quickly moving sails'.

venture Business speculation involving high profit and losses. A word frequently used in the play.

affections Feelings, thoughts.

Plucking the grass . . . wind Throwing grass in the air to see which way the wind blows. Remember that ships were dependent upon winds.

Piring Prying, looking.

roads Open harbours.

out of doubt Definitely.

ague Sickness (or sick with worry).

shallows . . . flats Very dangerous waters and sandbanks.

Andrew The name of a ship.

Vailing her high . . . her burial Vailing is bowing, and ribs are the sides of the ship. The high top is the top-sail. The image is that of a ship run aground on a sand bank.

straight Immediately.

And in a word . . . worth nothing? A recurring idea in the play: financially worth a lot at one moment, but the next moment being valueless.

To think on this i.e. the financial value.

Shall I have the thought . . . make me sad? All this may be a fantasy, but if true would make me very sad.

But tell not me Although this doesn't directly relate to me.

fortune Luck (as well as wealth).

bottom Ship.

nor is my whole estate In view of subsequent developments in the play

Antonio is deceiving himself and his friends, for he loses nearly all his possessions.

Not . . . neither A double negative emphasizing the idea of Antonio's being in love which, of course, he denies.

two-headed Janus The first of many classical references. Janus was a Roman God with two faces who guarded gates. One face was happy, the other frowning. Solanio's reference points to the appearance and reality theme in the play and its emphasis upon role-playing. Antonio must appear serious in order to obtain credit, yet his seriousness might be interpreted as genuine worry and anxiety. Important to the play are contrasts: happiness and sadness; wealth and poverty; friendship and isolation.

Nature hath . . . in her time Nature, life, has produced strange people.

peep through . . . eyes Laugh so much as to distort the face.

laugh like . . . bagpiper Parrots are associated with stupidity, and bagpipes with sadness, at which some people are foolish enough to laugh.

vinegar Sour, bitter i.e. the people who won't laugh at anything.

Nestor Greek leader at the siege of Troy noted for his longevity and wisdom – so, if he thinks it funny, it must be!

Here comes . . . Lorenzo The name order points to social importance: Bassanio, Antonio's 'kinsman' (a very close friend or relative of some kind) enters first – the others follow.

worth is very dear Key expressions in the play having a dual meaning: (a) financial value (b) emotional, regarded with affection.

embrace th' occasion Take the opportunity.

when shall we laugh? . . . it be so? When shall we all share a joke, must you become so unfriendly?

We'll make our . . . on yours When it's mutually convenient we'll get together.

I pray you have in mind . . . not fail you Perhaps Lorenzo is hinting to Bassanio that he plans to elope with Jessica.

too much respect (a) concern about (b) everybody looks up to you.

They lose it . . . with much care Too much worry is not good or healthy.

marvellously Incredibly. Said with irony in a negative fashion.

I hold the world . . . play a part A common idea of the world as a stage in which it is necessary to hide the real self and to act.

Let me play the fool . . . i.e. in life's play – continuing Antonio's metaphor of the previous line.

liver . . . wine An Elizabethan belief that wine-drinking warmed the liver.

heart cool . . . groans Sighing and groaning were believed to take blood from the heart.

mortifying Death-like.

his grandsire Like his grandfather's alabaster effigy.

Sleep when he wakes? Even when awake he seems to be asleep.

and creep . . . peevish? Make himself depressed by being irritable.

Do cream . . . standing pond In this image, the faces of these complacent men are compared to stagnating pools as they are covered with pale and acid expressions.

a wilful stillness entertain Keep silent.

With purpose . . . an opinion Deliberately to create a reputation.

profound conceit Deep understanding.

Sir Oracle The height of confidence and prudence.

O my Antonio . . . saying nothing Antonio, I know these people who by saying nothing pretend to be wise.

would almost . . . brothers fools If they spoke they would speak such folly that their listeners would think them foolish.

fool gudgeon . . . opinion A gudgeon is a very small fish used as bait. The reference is to an insignificant person trying to create an impression.

moe More.

gear What you say.

neat's tongue dried Literally, dried ox tongue.

maid not vendible An old maid.

It is that anything now Is there any sense in all that?

disabled Crippled in the financial sense.

showing a more . . . continuance i.e. I lived above my means. Shipping images (port) continued.

Nor do I now . . . a noble rate I am not now complaining that my living standards have to be reduced.

gag'd Pledged.

good Bassanio Valued in affectionate terms. Again a pun on the financial implications of an epithet of endearment.

if it stand . . . of honour Be regarded as honourable.

occasions Requirements. Whatever Bassanio requires that Antonio can supply is at his disposal.

shaft Arrow.

In my school-days . . . oft found both In my youth if I lost an arrow I'd shoot another one feathered and weighted the same in the same direction and by watching it very carefully in its flight, often found the first arrow.

or Either.

latter hazard Second arrow or loan which is put at risk. 'Hazard' occurs frequently, especially in relation to (a) Antonio's loan (b) Portia's caskets from which suitors must make a choice.

spend but . . . with circumstance Waste time with such circular arguments.

making questions . . . my uttermost In doubting that I will do my utmost for you.

prest unto it Prepared to do it.

sometimes Previously.

Cato . . . Portia Portia, the wife of Brutus, leader of those who killed
  Julius Caesar, noted for her bravery, wisdom, learning, and love of her
  husband. Her father Cato was from a distinguished Roman family and
  had a reputation for attacking corruption.

golden fleece . . . quest of her Another classical allusion. In mythology
  Jason retrieves the Golden Fleece – a fleece of pure gold kept at
  Colches (an area at the eastern end of the Black Sea). Portia at
  Belmont is a rich prize whom many nobles wish to obtain and possess.

rival place To compete as a rival.

presages Tells me.

thrift Luck, success.

fortunes Property. Again punning: (a) luck (b) happiness (c) property.

rack'd Pursued, tried.

I no question make Without any doubt.

To have . . . my sake On credit or from friendship.

Act I Scene 2

The scene moves from Venice to Belmont. Portia, an heiress,
discusses with her confidant Nerissa, why she is depressed. Her
father's will stipulates that the man who chooses the correct
casket i.e. the one which contains her portrait, from three of
gold, silver and lead, obtains Portia. She describes her suitors:
the Neapolitan prince is too fond of his horses; the Count from
the Rhineland is too gloomy; the Frenchman, Le Bon, too hypo-
critical; Falconbridge, the Englishman, too eccentric – and Portia's English is poor; the Scotsman is too bound up in his conflict
with England; the Duke of Saxony's nephew is a drunkard. If
these suitors represent the man who will choose the correct
casket then Portia hopes that she'll live to be an old maid.
Nerissa reminds her of Bassanio, whom she had found attractive. A messenger from yet another suitor arrives (in this
instance the Prince of Morocco).

Commentary

This is a scene of character and setting contrasts, of thematic
and plot development. Portia's future isn't dependent upon
trade, ships, the sea, or the weather. She is trapped by the
conditions of her father's will, and must wait for a choice to be
made. Like Antonio in Scene 1 she is depressed, and like him

has to be comforted by a friend. Gratiano has urged Antonio to be content. Nerissa, Gratiano's subsequent partner, urges her mistress Portia to be happy.

as sick that . . . starve with nothing To have too much is as bad as having too little.

mean Small.

seated in the mean Placed between the two (misery and good fortune).

superfluity comes . . . lives longer Having too much brings white hairs: those who have enough without excess live longer.

divine Churchman.

I can easier . . . own teaching It is easier to preach than to practise what one preaches.

the brain may . . . cold decree Moods were understood to depend upon four 'humours': blood, phlegm, choler, melancholy. Blood was regarded as the source of the passions i.e. the heart rules the head.

a hare is madness . . . the cripple The emotions of youth will ignore the wisdom of age, which may be restrictive.

reasoning Conversation.

is not in the fashion Not much help.

I may neither choose . . . dead father Portia is imprisoned by her dead father's will. Note the pun on 'will': (a) a binding legal document (b) desires, wishes.

thee A term of affection. Portia, socially Nerissa's superior, is emotionally close to her and confides in her.

over-name them Go over the suitors' list again.

level Point at.

colt An inexperienced young man. Note the horse imagery – Neapolitans were famed for their horsemanship.

appropriation Addition.

parts Self, attributes.

County Palatine Count from the Upper Rhine Land.

weeping philosopher Possibly a reference to the Greek philosopher Heraclitus of Ephesus (5th–4th century BC), whose pessimistic view of the human condition caused him to weep publically.

sadness Seriousness.

death's-head Skull.

by About.

every man in no man Lacks personality.

throstle Thrush.

falls straight a-cap'ring Immediately starts dancing.

If I should . . . twenty husbands He is so changeable that I'd be marrying twenty different men.

you will come into . . . in the English You will testify that I do not understand English: 'in the' echoes a foreigner speaking English.

proper man's picture Handsome, attractive.

dumb-show? Without understanding what he is saying.

round hose Short, puffed up breeches. Falconbridge's clothing is eccentric, being a mixture of Italian, French and German fashions.

neighbourly charity Meant ironically, for the Scot is feuding with the Englishman.

borrowed Was given. Possibly an allusion to Anglo-Scottish border troubles in 1596 – Scotland at the time was an independent state.

the Frenchman became ... for another A reference to the fact that the French frequently helped the Scots in their quarrels with England. They signed a mutual assistance agreement.

Vildly Vilely; this could also be an attempt to imitate the German 'v' and 'w' sounds.

the worst fall that ever fell When drunk he falls down. Portia will really be stooping very low indeed if she ends up with him.

deep Strong.

Rhenish wine Wine from the Rhine valley (see also Act III, Scene 1).

contrary Incorrect.

sponge Drunkard.

other sort Other way.

Sibylla Again a classical allusion, this time to the legendary old lady, whom Apollo promised should live as long as the sand grains she held in her hand.

Diana Roman Goddess of hunting, the moon, and virginity.

parcel Collection, group.

scholar and a soldier Ironic, since Bassanio is neither. Nerissa flatters him. She panders to what Portia wants to hear.

as I think so was he call'd She pretends to have forgotten his name so as not to appear too keen on him.

four strangers Six have been mentioned (Neapolitan, County Palatine, Le Bon, Falconbridge, Scottish lord, Duke of Saxony's nephew). Several explanations present themselves: (a) two have been to Belmont prior to the present scene (b) the Scottish and English lords were added to the scene to amuse the audience (c) the servant regards two of the suitors with such contempt that they are not even worth mentioning.

forerunner Messenger.

condition Character.

complexion of a devil Appearance, face. Of course the suitor is a Moor so will not have a white face and in referring to the 'devil' Shakespeare is expressing the fears of Venetian ladies. Racial intolerance and prejudice are major elements in this play.

shrive Hear my confession.

Act I Scene 3

Belmont and courtship give way to the harsh realities of the Venetian market place. Antonio is forced to borrow from a man he has insulted for years, Shylock. Shylock agrees to loan Antonio money not for interest, as is usual, but instead draws up a special agreement, a 'bond'. If Antonio cannot repay his debt in time Shylock will remove exactly one pound in weight of Antonio's flesh.

Commentary

The scene introduces Shylock, a central character and a focus of dramatic conflict in the play, Shylock versus Antonio, his friends and, by implication, Venetian society. It also brings to the fore the conflicts of religion and ideas. The clash between Antonio and Shylock is prefaced by the less hostile meeting between Bassanio and Shylock, although the subject of conversation is the same: money, interest, Antonio's honesty. Shylock views Antonio's financial security as too dispersed upon the unpredictable oceans. Shylock's social and religious differences come out in his reaction to Bassanio's invitation to dine with him. The meeting with Antonio is dominated by a conflict between religion, attitudes towards life, and personal animosity. Both draw upon scripture for their own purposes, both are concerned with security and money. It is important to realize that usury (money-lending) was seriously frowned upon by Catholicism and society. It was one of the few areas in which Jews were allowed to function but its practitioners were subject to personal insult.

Three thousand ducats A ducat was a Venetian gold coin. Inflation makes the sum in today's terms difficult to assess. One thing is certain – Bassanio requires a lot of money! Shylock's first entrance in the play is dramatically most effective.

be bound Act as surety, as guarantor.

well Understand, comprehend.

May you stead me? Will you help me?

a good man (a) financially secure (b) of honourable social status (c) morally upright.

his means are in supposition His financial soundness is in question.

argosy See note on p.19.

Tripolis Northern Lebanese port.

Indies Probably the New World, the Caribbean.

Rialto The centre of Venetian commercial life where information and gossip were exchanged, the Venetian equivalent of the City of London or Wall Street.

ventures See note on p.19.

squand'red abroad Uselessly scattered abroad. Shylock argues that Antonio has put too many eggs in too many different insecure baskets. He then outlines the dangers Antonio's goods have to face on the oceans.

pork Non-Kosher food, not eaten by Orthodox Jews.

habitation Food.

Your prophet the ... the devil into See Matthew, 8,8–34. Jesus casts devils into swine. Nazarite – a resident of Nazareth.

drink with you Wine has also to be Kosher.

fawning publican Several explanations have been offered, (a) a depressed Antonio is too friendly towards Bassanio (b) a reference to St Luke, 18,10–14 the parable of the insolent Pharisee and humble tax collector (publican) (c) he looks like a tax collector, being over polite when coming to collect!

low simplicity (a) foolishness (b) the depth of folly.

rate of usance Rates of interest charged on money.

Once upon the hip Metaphor from wrestling, referring to a position leading to a throw; a disadvantageous situation.

well-won thrift profits gained through exercising intelligence. Shylock has a totally different attitude to trading and business activities, which he regards as the application of high intelligence. Trade has no religious stigma for him.

Tubal A Biblical name, see Genesis, 10,2.

fair good (a) materially sound (b) morally upright.

Your worship was ... mouths i.e. we have just been talking about you.

ripe Urgent.

possess'd Been informed.

advantage Interest.

When Jacob graz'd ... Jacob's Shylock refers to Genesis, 30,31–43, a story of rivalry between brothers, where Jacob outwits Laban and secures for himself the strongest animals. It is a tale of high intelligence and skilled forward planning.

wise mother Genesis, 27,31–40: a reference to Rebecca, who obtained God's blessing for Jacob rather than Esau.

third possessor A reference to Jacob's three-fold plan, and to the fact that he represented the third generation (Isaac was his father, Abraham his father's father). By implication, Shylock is drawing attention to the longevity of Jewish history and experience.

interest? A three times repeated word and one cropping up throughout the play. Antonio uses it in the purely financial sense of money made on money lent. It has other meanings: (a) personal advantage (b) legal share (c) the focus of attention.

were compromis'd Reached an agreement.

eanlings New-born lambs.

being rank Ready for mating.

pill'd me Stripped: removed.

wands Sticks or rods used by shepherds.

fulsome Fat, strong.

eaning time Lambing season.

Fall Gave birth to.

serv'd for Acted as a servant. Antonio implies that skill and intelligence weren't involved.

inserted to make ... good? Mentioned in order to justify interest?

is your ... and rams? Shylock's financial wealth being but metal is literally unable to breed.

falsehood i.e. that which Antonio disagrees with.

rated Told me off, insulted me.

suff'rance Patience, hardship.

gaberdine A long cloak. Probably Jewish merchants in Venice wore particular costumes.

And all for ... mine own (a) because I put to use that which is my own.

Go to Come, come.

void your rheum ... my beard Spat on my beard.

foot me as you ... threshold Kick me as you would a stray dog at your door.

suit What you want.

bondsman's key In a slave's voice.

for when did ... of his friend? The classic example of anti-usury, i.e. when did one friend lend another money in order to make a financial profit?

But lend it ... the penalty It would be better for you to lend me the money as an enemy so that if I default, you can, without guilt or conscience, take your compensation.

stain'd me with Sullied my reputation.

doit A small insignificant sum. A doit was a small Dutch coin.

kind (a) generous (b) natural response to Antonio's comments on usury – Shylock says that he won't take interest from Antonio.

notary Special lawyer for drawing up contracts.

single bond Agreement signed only by you and with no extra conditions.

equal Exact, no more or less, a point seized upon by Portia (see Act IV, Scene 1).

break his day Fail to pay on the accepted date.

fearful Untrustworthy, unreliable. If Shylock is referring to Launcelot Gobbo, then he is absolutely right.

unthrifty Irresponsible.

The Hebrew will . . . grows kind (a) Shylock wishes to be a Christian and has consequently grown benevolent. (b) as Shylock is becoming kinder he'll develop into a Christian. The assumption is that all Christians are kind.
fair Reasonable.

Revision questions on Act I

1 How do Antonio's friends account for his sadness? How do *you* account for it?
2 What impressions from this act have you formed of the following: (a) Antonio (b) Shylock (c) Bassanio (c) Portia?
3 Describe Portia's suitors and discuss her opinion of them.
4 Analyse the first encounter in the play between Antonio and Shylock.
5 Compare and contrast the opening two scenes of the play (pay particular attention to characters, setting and images).

Act II Scene 1

This is set in Belmont and is the beginning of a series of short scenes. A Moroccan prince, one of Portia's suitors, presents himself to Portia. The prince thinks highly of himself, believing that he is extremely attractive to women.

Commentary

The themes of racial and religious differences continue, as does the play's emphasis upon gambling, games, and chance. Portia and her suitors are as subject to the lottery of the casket choice as are Antonio's and the other merchants' ships subject to the lottery of the high seas. Portia, if the Moroccan prince chooses correctly, will abide by the terms of her father's will and marry him. Hence the idea of marriage across racial and social and religious divides is introduced. Later Shylock's daughter, Jessica, elopes with Lorenzo.

tawny Moor Yellowish brown, not negroid. The Moroccan makes a grand, regal entrance.
shadowed Shaded.
livery Badge, sign.

Bring me . . . born He is attracted to fair complexions – to opposite features of his own.

Phoebus' The sun God.

blood is reddest A reference to a habit amongst youthful Elizabethan lads to demonstrate manliness by showing how red the blood is.

clime Country, i.e. Morocco.

hue Appearance.

Steal your thoughts Get you to be attracted to me.

scanted me Restricted, limited.

wit Will, commands.

Sophy Shah of Persia, Persian monarch.

Sultan Solyman Suleman the Magnificent, Turkish Sultan (1490–1566), continuously at war with Persia.

o'erstare Outstare.

Lichas Hercules' servant.

Which is the better . . . weaker hand i.e. the weaker man may yet defeat the stronger.

Alcides Another name for Hercules.

blind Fortune A reference to the goddess Fortune who was depicted as blindfolded – a symbol of the unaccountable and capricious variations in her dispensations to mankind.

Act II Scene 2

The scene is divided into three sections. In the first Launcelot Gobbo plays with his conscience and taunts his own father by pretending to be dead. He decides to leave Shylock's service. In the second, Launcelot meets Bassanio and enters his service. Bassanio prepares for his Belmont trip. In the third section Gratiano persuades Bassanio to let him go with him to Belmont.

Commentary

Underlying the ironic word-play and situational farce of the scene are serious elements: conscience; the loyalty of servant to master; false expectations; prejudice; the relationships of children to parents. Launcelot, with a conscience about leaving Shylock's service, exhibits racial prejudice, has false expectations about Bassanio's wealth, and cruelly torments his old father. Launcelot's disloyalty and attitude to his father are comparable to that of Jessica's to Shylock. Gratiano's jesting relationship with Bassanio parallels that of Nerissa's with Portia. Leonardo's fidelity to his master, Bassanio, provides an example of true master-servant relationships.

serve Permit.

fiend Devil, as in a morality play where a fight between good and evil takes place.

take the start Hurry up.

'Fia!' Away! From the Italian *via*.

Something smack, something grow to Had an appetite for the dishonest, or, liked other women apart from my mother.

God bless the mark God forgive me (for mentioning the devil). The 'mark' is probably the sign of the Cross.

saving your reverence With all due respect to you.

incarnation Red. Gobbo means incarnate (an example of what came to be known as a malapropism, after Sheridan's character Mrs Malaprop in *The Rivals*: the habit of misusing words, especially in confusing words similar in sounds. It is a basic comic device.)

sand-blind Partially blind.

gravel-blind Not totally without sight. Note the word-play in these phrases.

confusions The son deliberately sets out to confuse the father, who fails to recognize him.

marry Truly. A play on 'Mary': Launcelot cruelly gives his father nonsense directions.

sonties Idiom for 'saints'.

hard way to hit Difficult to find.

raise the waters Stir it up, annoy him.

Master Emphasized, as a reproof to his father for omitting his title.

well to live In fine shape.

a He.

ergo Therefore (Lat.).

Master A play on the word. The father refuses to give his son the title, but offers it to a stranger in the street when he greets him.

father Irony, (a) a common form of address to an old man (b) in this case the father hasn't recognized the son.

fates and destinies . . . Sisters Three In Greek mythology the three Goddesses of Fate: one held the spindle; the second spun man's fate upon the spindle; the third cut the thread which represented life. Note the difference between Launcelot's fairly educated references and the poor circumstances of the father and son.

sayings Maxims, short phrases with a moral intent.

hovel-post The support in a very poor dwelling.

thou Gobbo, once he has recognized his own son, changes from the formal 'you' to the more personal 'thou'.

fill-horse Horse which draws carts or heavy loads.

set up my rest Staked everything, finally decided: from an Elizabethan card game.

a halter! A rope to hang himself with.

tell Count.

finger I have ... ribs Launcelot reverses the order, thus achieving a comic effect.

rare new liveries Expensive new servants' clothing. Evidently Bassanio's new-found wealth (i.e. Antonio's, borrowed from Shylock) is already servants' gossip.

liveries to making See about the new costumes (needed to impress Portia).

To him father Pantomime farce: the old man goes first, then the son, then the old man, then the son, and so on.

Gramercy Many thanks.

specify State, testify – this begins a sequence of misusing words.

infection Affection, desire, although could also be taken literally.

short and the long is A reversal for comic effect of the expression 'the long and the short'.

scarce cater-cousins Hardly close friends.

frutify Confirm, certify.

dish of doves A present of doves, for eating.

impertinent Relevant, pertinent, a comic misuse of language.

defect Nature, effect.

old proverb i.e. 'The grace of God is wealth enough'. 2 Corinthians, 12,9.

a livery/More guarded Decorated clothing.

well if any man ... good fortune Note how Launcelot's mistaken use of 'any' (it should be 'no') reverses his intended meaning.

simple line of life Palmists claimed to tell fortunes from lines on the hands (the 'life-line', the 'heart-line' etc).

simple coming-in Modest allowance.

to scape ... my life Possibly an allusion to the catalogue of perils outlined in 2 Corinthians, 11,25–6: 'Thrice was I beaten with rods ...'

the edge of a feather-bed (a) the threat of marriage (b) a feather-bed has no edges!

gear Purpose.

bestowed i.e. on board the ship for Belmont.

allay Restrain.

misconst'red Misjudged.

habit Appearance.

demurely Seriously.

hood cover.

sad ostant Sad appearance and behaviour.

To please his grandam The behaviour will please even his grandmother.

Act II Scene 3

Launcelot's farewell to Jessica is a tearful affair. She asks him to take a message to Lorenzo. Left alone, Jessica expresses the conflict between her relationship with her father and her love for Lorenzo.

Commentary

The scene focusses upon relationships between children and parents, servants and mistresses. Jessica believes that her relationship with Lorenzo will reduce the religious tension in Venice. Launcelot is so overcome with emotion that he cannot speak. Throughout the play feelings and emotions are conveyed in words having double meanings which relate commercial value to personal value. Launcelot's tears are genuine – he is truly fond of Jessica.

some taste of tediousness The element of boredom.
exhibit Stop.
foolish drops i.e. tears.
heinous Hateful.

Act II Scene 4

In a Venetian street Gratiano, Lorenzo, Salerio and Solanio prepare for Bassanio's going away party. Launcelot arrives with Jessica's letter for Lorenzo. Bassanio sends a dinner invitation to Shylock for that evening. Launcelot leaves with a further message for Jessica. Lorenzo reveals that he has a torch-bearer for the masque, and agrees to meet the others later at Gratiano's house. He then tells Gratiano of the elopement plans. Jessica dressed as a page will leave Shylock's house with jewels and money and act as Lorenzo's torch-bearer.

Commentary

Disguise, frivolity, games, plans provide a contrast to the serious business world of Venice, and to Portia's round of suitors opening caskets. Launcelot as messenger links the world of Shylock and Jessica with that of Bassanio and Lorenzo. One of the plots develops: Jessica initiates her journey from one world to another, taking her possessions with her (or rather her father's goods). She is described as 'gentle' and 'fair', although to her father she would appear as neither.

in During.
Disguise us . . . in an hour They are going to dress up for the masque or fancy-dress ball.
torch-bearers These are hired to accompany party-goers.
quaintly ordered Properly arranged.
furnish us Prepare ourselves.
it shall please . . . to signify It seems that you will gain further information.
break up this Remove the seals on the letter.
in faith . . . fair hand A play on (a) religious belief (b) beauty (c) honesty (d) financial value.
Hold here – take this Wait a minute. Lorenzo gives him another message, and perhaps tips him.
gentle Perhaps a pun on Gentile, a non-Jew.
issue Daughter.

Act II Scene 5

Shylock tells Jessica to lock up the house whilst he goes to Bassanio's for supper. Shylock fears that all is not well. Launcelot gives Jessica Lorenzo's message. Shylock reflects upon how pleased he is to be rid of Launcelot, and also Bassanio's financial insecurity. Left alone Jessica bids farewell to her father.

Commentary

Notice the irony in this scene. Shylock's forebodings are correct. The audience is shown Jessica at home and her father's absolute trust in her, which serves to heighten her betrayal. Shylock's hatred for Venetian society further emerges, as does his intense dislike of pleasure. He acts inconsistently. Remember that in Act I, Scene 3 he strongly rejected Bassanio's offer to dine with him. Now he accepts out of self-interest, revenge and hate. Shylock is preoccupied with his possessions, of which Jessica is one. Also evident is Launcelot's intelligence and inventiveness: he manages to get the message to Jessica and plays on Shylock's superstitious nature.

gormandize Stuff yourself with food – overeat. A contradiction of Launcelot's comment in Act II, Scene 2 that Shylock has starved his household.

rend apparel out Wear clothes out quickly.

bid forth Asked out.

dream of money-bags to-night Dreamt of money last night – regarded as a sign of bad luck to come.

reproach Approach. However, should Shylock's plot against Antonio succeed, he (Shylock) might well expect Bassanio's reproach.

And they have conspired together i.e. arranged a masque. Dramatic irony – Launcelot, Jessica and the audience are aware that other plans are under way.

Black-Monday Launcelot plays on Shylock's superstitious nature by referring to the Easter Monday of 1360 when Edward III's army was caught in the fog and cold outside Paris. Many soldiers froze to death.

six o'clock . . . was four year Time of course is of the essence in Jessica's elopement plans.

wry-neck'd fife Whilst playing the curved flute, the player turned the face away from the instrument.

varnish'd faces Painted, disguised with masks.

shallow fopp'ry Superficial stupidity: Shylock gives here a superb dismissive description full of contempt for what is going on around him.

Jacob's staff The sign of his strength. Genesis, 32,10: 'For with my staff I passed over this Jordan; and now I am become two bands.' Shylock is asking for strength.

worth a Jewes eyes i.e. Lorenzo will be worth more than a Jew. A reference to Jewish financial payments made in medieval times in order to escape having an eye removed. This unpleasant comment is made to Jessica in an aside as Launcelot leaves.

Hagar's offspring Hagar, a Gentile Egyptian gave birth to Ishmael, Abraham's son who was outcast (Genesis, 16).

patch Fool. Refers to part of the clown's traditional multi-coloured patched costume.

Snail-slow in profit He works very slowly.

More than the wild cat The wild cat sleeps through the day and is active at night.

drones hive They sucked honey from the beehive.

borrowed purse i.e. Bassanio's money from Antonio borrowed from Shylock.

crost i.e. nothing goes wrong with the plans.

Act II Scene 6

Jessica leaves her father's house dressed as a page to elope with Lorenzo, taking some of Shylock's possessions with her. At the end of the scene Antonio says that due to a change in the winds, Bassanio will leave for Belmont sooner than anticipated.

Commentary

The emphasis is on Jessica and Lorenzo and their mutual desires, which bridge religious and cultural divisions. There is a lot of punning in the scene, with sexual innuendos highlighting human sexual union. However, reference to bonds, to exchange, possessions, promises, regrets, and the unpredictable, ensure that other dramatic elements are not lost sight of.

penthouse Porch or roof projecting into the street. Probably the upper stage balcony.

Venus' pigeons fly Doves are said to have drawn the Goddess of Love's chariot. 'Pigeons' could mean also lovers.

To seal love's . . . new made To consummate their recently sworn love. Note 'bonds' with its many implications in the play.

keep obliged faith unforfeited! To abide faithfully to a contract, or be faithful whilst married.

untread again Retrace.

all things that . . . enjoy'd To imagine something is better than actually experiencing it.

younger Young nobleman.

prodigal Over-spender, waster. Cf. Prodigal Son parable in Luke, 15,11–32. See also note on Act II, Scene 5.

scarfed bark A ship decked out with flags and bunting.

strumpet wind! (a) the free, unrestrained winds (b) the wind is personified as a prostitute – the Prodigal Son went to many different prostitutes.

over-weather'd ribs Damaged by the weather: 'ribs' refers to (a) the Prodigal Son (b) the wrecked ship.

abode Delay.

play the thieves for wives i.e. start stealing in order to get a wife. Perhaps this comment indicates that Lorenzo's conscience is troubled by his actions?

my father Jew Shylock is to be his father-in-law.

thy thoughts Your love and desire for me.

my exchange (a) change into page-boy's clothes (b) remorse for leaving her father and removing his possessions.

Cupid The God of love, depicted as blind.

goodsooth Truly, really.

too too light i.e. torches and candles but also 'light' behaviour. Jessica is ashamed of being dressed as a boy.

office of discovery As it is revealed.
garnish Costume.
doth play the runaway Is quickly disappearing.
stay'd for Expected.
by my hood An oath. Gratiano may be wearing a hood.
Beshrew me Let ill luck come upon me. Also a reference to a 'shrew' or
very difficult woman.
but I However.

Act II Scene 7

Back at Belmont, with much ceremonial formality, the Moroccan Prince chooses one of the three caskets in order to win
Portia. His choice is the gold casket, which has a skull inside it.

Commentary

The scene is concerned with value and its message is contained
within the rhyming couplets the Moroccan Prince finds in the
gold casket: 'All that glisters is not gold.' He mistakes outward
appearance for inner worth and value. Portia awaits her fate
with dignity. The Prince behaves with the utmost nobility. The
emphasis upon the colours gold, silver and lead draws attention
to the scene's visual aspects. The caskets are allegorical (an
allegory is a representation of an abstract or spiritual meaning
through using concrete or material forms, here, caskets): within
each casket is a message.

several Different.
who Which.
blunt A pun on: (a) basic (b) sharp, direct.
withal As well.
fair advantages Of gaining well. In view of what happens in the play,
an ironic comment.
golden Rich, noble.
dross Baseness, lowliness.
And weigh thy value ... even hand Judge carefully. Human choice is
determined by the weight of precious metals.
If thou be'st rated by thy estimation If you are judged according to the
way in which you judge yourself.
weak disabling Not doing oneself justice.
mortal breathing saint i.e. Portia. Lovers seeking the lady of their
desires were often compared to pilgrims searching for their saint or
for faith.

Hyrcanian The land to the south of the Caspian Sea noted for its
wildness and untamed tigers.

vasty Huge expanse.

too gross . . . grave She, Portia, wouldn't be buried in such cheap
clothing.

rib Close.

cerecloth Cloth in which bodies are wrapped for burial.

try'd gold Genuine, tested gold.

A coin that bears . . . insculp'd upon A golden coin prominently
displaying the figure of St Michael fighting the dragon. The Prince
judges by surface appearances!

form Picture.

carrion Death A skull representing death.

Gilded Those richly and ornately decorated.

complexion A pun (a) way of thinking (b) physical appearance.

Act II Scene 8

Back in Venice Salerio and Solanio talk of Shylock's anger on
discovering Jessica's elopement and the loss of the jewels. They
also describe Antonio's sorrow at Bassanio's departure.

Commentary

The audience is told about, rather than shown, two emotional
situations. Shylock is distraught by his losses: emotional and
financial distress are closely interwoven. Salerio and Solanio also
observe that a Venetian ship has run aground on the English
Channel coast. They hope that the ship isn't Antonio's because
in his present mood Shylock will insist upon revenge. Shylock's
personal loss is paralleled by Antonio's loss of Bassanio. The
scene illustrates the close association throughout the play
between human feelings, judgement, and financial worth: 'bond'
and 'business' are ever-present.

Let good Antonio . . . his day The highly regarded Antonio had better
make sure that he pays Shylock back at the correct time. Again this is a
play on the word 'good'.

reason'd Gossiped.

narrow seas . . . and English i.e. the English Channel.

fraught laden.

Slubber not Don't rush.

stay the very riping of the time Until it is the right time.

your mind of love Your mind, which is full of love for Portia.

ostents Displays. Antonio seems unaware of the casket challenge.
I think he only loves . . . for him Antonio judges everything in terms of his all-consuming love for Bassanio.
quicken Cheer up.
embraced heaviness Depression caused by losing Bassanio.

Act II Scene 9

At Belmont the Prince of Arragon tries his luck at the caskets and chooses the silver one which contains an idiot's head. A messenger announces that a Venetian has arrived to try his luck.

Commentary

This is another formal allegorical scene. Arragon appears with servants and cornets. The casket ritual unfolds. Silver stands for self-deception, vanity and conceit. Again the scene revolves around valuation, and the second act concludes on a note of expectation: Portia and Nerissa await the new suitor; Venice awaits Shylock's anger and the fate of Antonio's ships.

election presently Make his choice immediately.
Not learning more than . . . doth teach Being misled by appearances.
martlet A bird which builds its nest in dangerous, exposed places which appear to be safe.
force and road of casualty Most likely to be blown down – compare with the ships which are subject to the unpredictable weather.
jump with . . . spirits Be the same as ordinary people.
To cozen Fortune To cheat fate or fortune.
Without the stamp of merit? Seal or mark of approval. He will not attempt to gain what he doesn't deserve.
cover that stand bare! To cover the head was a sign of respect and honour. So, he comments that those who are now masters will now remove their hats, and those who are honest servants will cover their heads.
How much low peasantry . . . new-varnish'd If virtue and truth were the values respected, then many peasants and poor people would be chosen for high positions.
chaff Cast aside; literally – discarded wheat husks.
new-varnish'd Given a fresh coat: socially restored or renewed.
assume desert Take what I think I deserve.
blinking idiot An imbecile's head.
To offend and judge . . . offices . . . natures Arragon agreed to the terms. Now that the choice has been a negative one he questions the terms he agreed to.

shadows illusions, dreams.
Iwis Definitely.
Silver'd o'er (a) wealthy (b) old (i.e. with silver hair).
sped Dismissed, finished.
Thus hath the . . . the moth i.e. Arragon has been punished just as a
  moth is injured when it flies into the flame of a candle.
deliberate With too much thought rather than instinct.
wit Intelligence, i.e. are too clever.
sensible regrets Not only words but gifts as well.
commends Compliments and greetings.
fore-spurrer Messenger.
anon Before long.
high-day wit Exaggerated compliments.
Cupid's post Love's messengers.

Revision questions on Act II

1 Write a description of the casket scenes in this act. What do
you think is the significance of each scene?
2 What have you learned in this act about the relationship
between Shylock and Jessica?
3 What is Launcelot Gobbo's role in this act?
4 Briefly describe the parts played by two of the following in Act
II: (a) Gratiano (b) Bassanio (c) Solanio and Salerio.
5 Write a brief account of Jessica's elopement.

Act III Scene 1

In Venice Solanio and Salerio gossip about Antonio's ship
having run aground on the Goodwin sands. Shylock, distracted
by his daughter's behaviour, and taunted by Solanio, makes one
of the most powerful speeches in the play about common universal humanity. Tubal confirms the news of Antonio's losses,
and Shylock takes comfort in revenge.

Commentary

Solanio's and Salerio's jibes and Shylock's powerful plea 'Hath not
a Jew eyes?' draw attention to an important aspect of the play –
religious and racial intolerance. However, at times Shylock is a
comic figure more concerned with the loss of his jewelry than his
daughter and with how much the search for her is costing him.
He eagerly seizes upon revenge on Antonio as some kind of

compensation for his wrongs. Notice how words with both financial and emotional meaning are prominent: does Shylock's ring
that his wife gave him mean more to him than his actual
daughter – or is it the ring's associations that move him so much?
In this scene the Antonio-Bassanio-Shylock plot centering upon
the bond, and the Jessica-Lorenzo-Shylock plot centering upon
her elopement, interweave. Jessica's actions provoke Shylock
into his reaction.

it lives there uncheck'd Is the same as ever.
Goodwins The dangerous sands close to the Isle of Thanet in Kent.
knapp'd Bites.
without any slips of prolixity i.e. without beating about the bush.
Come, the full stop i.e. get on with it, what is the point you wish to
  make?
cross my prayer Interfere with; with perhaps an echo of the
  crucifixion.
knew the tailor that . . . withal Knew the tailor who made her page's
  disguise.
bird was flidge i.e. Jessica was restless and ready to leave home.
complexion Natural.
dam Nest, home, mother.
damn'd A pun on the meanings of 'dam' and the sense of being cursed.
devil may be her judge i.e. judged by non-Christian standards.
carrion Rotting piece of flesh.
rebels it at these years? i.e. what right have you at your age to object, to
  rebel against that which is natural?
Rhenish White wine. Conveys the idea of Shylock's feeble blood and
  Jessica's strong, youthful red blood. See also Act I, Scene 2, where
  Portia refers to 'Rhenish wine'.
bad match Bad bargain. Shylock's mind links Antonio with Jessica.
cur'sy Courtesy i.e. he lent money without interest as an act of charity.
hind'red me half a million Cost me a lot of money.
dimensions Limbs.
we will resemble you in that Notice that Shylock draws attention to
  basic human elements which transcend ethnic, religious, and social
  differences. People have feelings, passions, are sensitive, and bleed;
  when wronged they wish to take revenge.
what is his humility? How should he behave?
sufferance be Reaction be.
The villainy you teach . . . go hard I will behave in the harsh way that
  you have behaved and follow the examples you have set.
a third cannot be match'd Cannot be found to compare with Shylock
  and Tubal.
Frankfort There were twice yearly fairs in Frankfurt, Germany.

the curse Possibly a reference to Deuteronomy, 28,15–68 or Daniel, 9,11, examples of curses in the Old Testament.

hears'd at my foot In her coffin. Shylock is beside himself with grief.

what's spent i.e. in terms of time, energy and money.

I thank thee good Tubal . . . good news To Shylock in his despair news of Antonio's loss comes as something of a relief.

but break (a) become bankrupt (b) personally suffer (c) i.e. break the bond.

turquoise A very expensive, rare, precious stone of light blue colouring.

Leah i.e. his dead wife. See Genesis, 29,16–21. Leah was the only one of Jacob's wives to have a daughter. Leah was Laban's daughter (see Act I, Scene 3); Jacob preferred her sister Rachel.

wilderness of monkeys A marvellous image; notice the hyperbole (overstatement), the contradiction (wilderness – full of monkeys).

fee me Find me; also in the financial sense of, give the officer a fee to come.

bespeak him a fortnight before Find an officer a fortnight before the bond is due (so that Antonio can immediately be arrested).

for were he out . . . I will With him out of the way, I can make what profits I like.

Act III Scene 2

Venice and Belmont are linked. Bassanio, probably with non-verbal help from Portia, chooses the correct casket. He wins Portia, and Gratiano also declares his love for Nerissa. Lorenzo and Jessica arrive with Salerio to announce the loss of Antonio's ships. Bassanio tells Portia that Antonio entered into a bond with Shylock out of love for him (Bassanio). Portia agrees to pay the debt, and advises Bassanio that as soon as they are married he should return to Venice to settle the matter.

Commentary

This scene, uniting two worlds, is divided into two. Portia guides Bassanio's choice which will prove to be an illustration of natural love rather than one based on wealth and riches. The setting, stage props (the caskets), use of words and actions, all emphasize the contrast between the genuine, the natural, and the artificial. Bassanio's faithfulness is pledged with a ring – the later loss of which will cause him much embarrassment (note that the significance of rings has been reinforced in the last scene through

Shylock's passion about the loss of Leah's ring). Gratiano's and Nerissa's love complements that of their master and mistress. The entry of a third couple, Lorenzo and Jessica, with Salerio, disturbs the excited atmosphere and the lines of sexual jesting. We are back to Venice and its problems. Bassanio's trip to Belmont has been purchased at Antonio's expense. Bassanio has gambled and won, Antonio gambled and lost. Shylock will have his bond, his revenge. Jessica, his daughter, also wants revenge upon her father. Portia suggests a solution.

(but it is not love) Portia doesn't wish to openly confess to Bassanio that she loves him.

Hate counsels ... a quality It isn't hate which gives you such advice.

quality Manner.

yet a maiden ... thought Traditionally a maiden has only her thoughts; she is unable to express her wishes.

some month or two The 'few days' of the opening lines have now become months.

I am forsworn ... I had been forsworn I am unable to break my oath; if you make the wrong choice I'll wish I had done so.

Beshrew Cover.

o'erlook'd me Entranced.

naughty Difficult, wicked. A much stronger word then than now.

yours, not yours Yours by feelings of love, but not yours because of the will (unless the right choice is made).

Let Fortune ... I Let Fortune be damned if our love is stopped.

to peise the time To weigh time, i.e. to draw out/lengthen.

eche it Delay it: put off the final decision.

the rack An instrument of torture.

What treason The rack was used in treason cases: it literally stretched its victims until they confessed. Bassanio and Portia desire each other; for Portia to give way would be to commit treason to her father's wishes. Emotionally, in terms of tension and frustration, Bassanio and she are both 'upon the rack'.

fear th' enjoying Afraid that I will not be able to enjoy my love (because he may make the wrong choice).

amity Friendship and co-relationship.

There may as well ... and my love Just as fire and snow cannot co-exist, nor can treason live with Bassanio's love for Portia, i.e. he is true and loyal.

If you do ... find me out Portia has faith that the person who truly loves here will make the right choice (see also Act I, Scene 2 Nerissa 1.31–2).

swan-like A traditional poetic image referring to the old belief that a swan sings once – before it dies.

stand more proper Be more appropriate.

as the flourish . . . monarch At coronations trumpets announce the crowning of a new monarch.

dulcet sounds Sweet sounds.

Alcides Alcides (Hercules) rescued Hesione, daughter of the Trojan King Laomedon, from being sacrificed to a sea-monster. He acted not from love but from a desire to possess the horses offered as a reward. Portia sees herself as Hesione and Bassanio as an Alcides acting out of love.

The rest aloof . . . Dardanian . . . exploit Nerissa and the other servants also observe what is happening as did the Dardanian (Trojan) women, as they watched Alcides rescue Hesione.

Live thou, I live (a) If you should live I will live (b) If you make the right choice my life will be a better one.

A song . . . to himself Whilst Bassanio examines the caskets music and song accompany him. It has been suggested that the song's lyrics with the rhymes 'bred', 'head', 'nourished' might suggest to Bassanio the word 'lead'. On the other hand, such a hint could be regarded as cheating. Bassanio's intuitive love must come from within, be genuine, and not spoilt by prompting.

where is Fancy bred? Where is passing affection developed as opposed to real true love?

So may . . . themselves The message of the song is 'don't let appearances deceive you'.

season'd with . . . the show of evil? Irony – the better the lawyer the more likely his guilty client is to get away with the crime. Notice that Portia in the next act will use 'a gracious voice' to help Bassanio and Antonio.

grossness That which is wrong.

stairs of sand This is powerful poetry. Think how difficult it is to hold sand in the hand and how easily it gives way underfoot.

Mars The Roman god of war.

Who inward . . . white as milk? Appear to be brave but in fact are cowards. The liver was thought of as the seat of the affections.

valour's excrement Assume only the outward signs of courage (*excrement*: outgrowth, such as a beard).

To render them redoubted Make them feared.

purchas'd by the weight i.e. can be bought by the use of cosmetics.

a miracle in nature Those naturally not born attractive become so.

crisped snaky . . . locks Probably a reference to the fashion at the time for 'golden' hair – as the Queen was fair-headed. The curly locks may be tempting but they are also dangerous: the allusion is of course to the serpent in the Garden of Eden who tempted Adam.

dowry of a second head A wig.

bred them in the sepulchre Now dead and buried.

ornament i.e. jewelry, make-up.

guiled shore . . . dangerous sea Another reference to the dangers of shipping – an attractive sea-shore may in fact be a most dangerous one. By implication, so may an attractive casket or a pretty face.

an Indian beauty Dark skins were not regarded as attractive at the time (see above).

Hard food for Midas Midas was given the power to transform all that he touched into gold: no exception was made for food. He therefore begged the God Bacchus, who had given him the power, to take it back again.

thee thou pale Bassanio refers to the silver casket.

common drudge Silver usually contained in coins.

rash-embrac'd despair Thinking about unpleasant things before they actually occur.

moderate Relax. Portia knows he has chosen the right casket.

allay Calm.

In measure Moderately.

I surfeit It becomes too much.

counterfeit Picture.

riding on the balls of mine Looking directly into mine eyes.

sunder Part.

having made one . . . unfurnish'd Having painted one eye the artist would be so dazzled by it that he'd be unable to paint the other.

shadow Portrait. Note the antithesis between 'substance' and 'shadow'.

continent That which contains.

Chance as fair (a) you have chosen correctly (b) fairly.

hold your fortune for your bliss Keep what you have obtained for your happiness.

by note (a) by what is written in the casket (b) an account – money (c) as in the bond.

confirm'd . . . by you Until fully agreed by you. Notice the continuation of financial imagery.

account (a) eyes, sight, vision (b) opinion (c) financial reckoning (of course marriage to Portia will solve all Bassanio's financial problems).

livings Property brought with me as dowry.

to term in gross To count up without considering deductions.

unlesson'd (a) not been properly taught (b) inexperienced (in the sexual sense and in the sense of not being taught how to look after a husband).

than this In this, being aware of.

presage Be.

Vantage Chance. Indeed, later in the play Portia, as Balthasar, tests Bassanio by removing his ring.

exclaim on you Protest against you.

Where every something . . . not express'd Everything becomes confused, expressing only a general state of happiness.

when this ring . . . dead! Portia may well take Bassanio at his word!

This remark will rebound on Bassanio in the last scene of the play, when she accuses him of having given it away.

wish none for me (a) you are so happy you don't really need my good wishes (b) you don't wish me not to be happy also.

bargain Agreement. Again notice how commercial language is used to express human emotions.

my very roof i.e. his mouth.

so you stand pleas'd If you approve.

We'll play with them ... ducats Bet you a thousand ducats we have a boy before you do!

infidel Non-Christian, i.e. Jessica.

If that youth of ... bid you welcome Assuming that my newly gained authority here gives me the right to welcome you first.

his estate (a) how he is (pun on 'state') (b) how his financial fortunes are.

Nerissa, cheer ... her welcome i.e. look after Jessica.

Jasons, we have ... the fleece See Act I, Scene 2. Remember that 'fleece' is a pun on 'fleet', an idea continued in Salerio's comment.

shrewd Unpleasant.

dear (a) close friend in terms of feelings (b) rich friend – in financial terms.

Could turn so much ... man Change the facial appearance and expression of a normally well-balanced sane person.

mere deadly.

feed my means Give me financial support. Notice the powerful metaphor 'feed' with its meaning of eating and being eaten.

not one hit? Not one success?

Barbary The North African Mediterranean coast.

And not one vessel ... marring rocks? Didn't one of his ships avoid the dangers experienced at sea?

present money Money needed now.

confound Destroy, ruin.

plies Contact, petition.

impeach Challenge, question.

magnificoes Nobles.

Of greatest port Of highest rank. Notice that 'port' also relates to shipping.

best-condition'd Best natured.

unwearied spirit Never tired of doing favours.

ancient Roman honour The Roman values of pride and dignity.

deface the bond Cancel it.

merry cheer Happy face.

dear bought ... love you dear Note the punning on 'dear' – financially expensive and beloved emotionally. The meaning is: since it has cost a lot (emotionally and financially) for us to be together, my love for you will reflect that cost.

use your pleasure Suit yourself.
be interposer Interfere.

Act III Scene 3

Back in Venice, the time to pay Shylock's debt has arrived. Antonio is imprisoned and attempts unsuccessfully to speak with a revengeful Shylock.

Commentary

Again the two are contrasted and the cause of their dispute highlighted. Shylock is deranged and obsessed, Antonio all too reasonable for a man deeply in debt. The words 'bond', 'money' and 'trade' pre-dominate.

good Notice the two meanings: (a) a honourable person (b) financially sound.
naughty Wicked (see note, p.42).
dull-ey'd (a) tearful (b) short-sighted (c) over-sensitive.
It is the most Notice that Shylock is reduced to an object.
kept with Lived with.
bootless prayers Pointless prayers.
his forfeitures Penalties due to him.
commodity (a) conveniences (b) trading rights.
impeach Throw doubt upon. See also note p.45.
Since that the trade . . . nations i.e. Venetian prosperity, its trade, depends upon people from all nations.
bated me (a) depressed me (b) caused me to lose weight (because of worry).

Act III Scene 4

The action moves once again to Belmont, where Portia sets in motion her plan to assist Antonio. She leaves Lorenzo and Jessica in charge of her house and sends her servant Balthasar to Padua for information from the legal expert Doctor Bellario. Portia tells Nerissa that they will dress up as male pages, and on the way to Venice she'll disclose the rest of the plan to her.

Commentary

Portia in this scene is in command. The emphasis is upon the themes of loyalty and fidelity to friends, disguise and deceit. There are many sexual allusions at the end of the scene.

conceit Appearance, bearing, understanding.

god-like amity Friendship. A reference to an idea current at the time that friendship was a God-given gift.

lover Close, bosom-friend.

Than customary bounty ... you Than your natural kindness makes you.

converse Meet.

egall Equal.

bosom Close. Note that Portia doesn't show any jealousy of the friendship between Bassanio and Antonio.

semblance of my soul i.e. Antonio.

husbandry Arranging.

deny this imposition Refuse this duty.

Padua About twenty miles from Belmont. There was a Law School in Padua.

imagin'd speed As fast as you can.

traject Ferry.

habit Dress.

accomplished/With that we lack Possess what we haven't got. There is a sexual innuendo here – they will think that we are sexually experienced. Remember that they will be disguised as young men!

accoutered Dressed up.

prettier More elegant.

braver grace Bolder appearance.

speak between ... and boy As a boy whose voice is just breaking.

reed voice Thin, treble sounding note.

mincing Feminine.

quaint Clever.

I could not do withal There was nothing that I could do about it.

puny Silly, small.

will practise Portia describes her own disguise and the tricks she is going to play. Remember that women didn't perform on the stage. She is going to dress as a boy. In reality her part was played by a male, so there is a double irony underlying her speech.

measure twenty miles to-day Either (a) to Bellario in Padua, or (b) directly to Venice. The text is unclear on where exactly they go first of all.

Act III Scene 5

Lorenzo's control over Portia's household is somewhat chal-lenged by Launcelot's verbal quibbling. This scene is not merely a preparation for the final scene of the play. Launcelot Gobbo's racially biased quips introduce a note of sourness into the pre-viously happy Belmont atmosphere. His verbal dexterity reveals that he is more than a mere word player.

Commentary

Images of food, legitimacy and illegitimacy are prominent in a scene in which Jessica appears repressed. She is disturbed by Launcelot's innuendoes, has become a Christian and entered into a new strange world.

the sins of the father . . . children A reference to Moses' teachings –
  Exodus, 20,5: 'I the Lord thy God *am* a jealous God visiting the
  iniquity of the fathers upon the children unto the third and fourth
  generation of them that hate me.'
Scylla . . . Charybdis In Homer's *Odyssey*, Scylla is the rock or six-
  headed monster, and Charybdis the whirlpool. Sailors tried to sail
  between the two. Launcelot is in fact insulting Jessica by identifying
  her father with Scylla and her mother with Charybdis.
gone both ways Damned whatever you do.
I shall be sav'd Cf. Corinthians, 7,14: 'the unbelieving wife is sanctified
  by the husband.'
enow Enough.
pork-eaters Cf. Shylock's comment in Act I, Scene 3 in reply to
  Antonio's invitation to dine with him. Launcelot refers to the Jewish
  laws against pork-eating. He is laughing at them.
are out have disagreed.
I shall answer . . . by you Launcelot! There may have been a topical
  reference here which is now lost. Venice was a multi-racial city. The
  general meaning is 'I shall provide children for the common good,
  whereas you have made the Moor pregnant, Launcelot.' Remember
  that throughout the scene Launcelot has continually played upon
  Jessica's nerves with his references to her former religious background
  and upbringing.
It is much that the Moor . . . took her for Launcelot half-apologizes but
  answers back by commenting that he thought that the pregnant Moor
  was a prostitute.
I think the best grace . . . parrots Lorenzo sarcastically tells Launcelot
  off for his foolish punning. He says it will soon be polite to say

nothing, and speech by chatterers only will be approved.

wit-snapper i.e. quibbler. Note the implied meaning of (a) eating (b) referring to a certain kind of bird snapping at fish.

'cover' Lay the table.

quarrelling with occasion! Arguing for the sake of doing so.

humours and conceits Moods and temper.

dear discretion Lorenzo is being sarcastic: what 'nice' distinctions Gobbo makes! How clever he thinks he is!

Garnish'd Supplied.

Defy the matter Avoid the real meaning.

how cheer'st thou Jessica? How are things with you?

very meet very appropriate.

Pawn'd Staked.

a stomach (a) desire to (b) appetite.

Then howsome'er ... digest it However you talk about me at least good food will help me to take it.

Revision questions on Act III

1 Why does Bassanio choose the 'lead' casket?

2 Why is Shylock so angry?

3 What role does Portia play in this act?

4 Briefly describe the parts played by two of the following in this act: (a) Antonio (b) Solanio (c) Jessica (d) Launcelot Gobbo (e) Lorenzo.

5 Compare and contrast scenes in this act set in Venice and Belmont.

Act IV Scene 1

This great scene is divided into five sections. In the first the Duke sympathizes with Antonio. The second section concentrates on Shylock, who refuses pleas of mercy from the Duke. Shylock argues that Venetian law would be a farce if his rights are not upheld. Bassanio tries to argue with Shylock but is stopped by Antonio, who is convinced that his enemy will show no mercy. Bassanio's offer of three times the sum owed falls on deaf ears. The Duke seems to have no alternative but to conceed to Shylock's demands. In the third section Nerissa, acting as Portia's confidant, prepares the way for her appearance whilst Gratiano insults Shylock.

The fourth section witnesses the supreme dramatic confrontation between the young lawyer (i.e. Portia) and Shylock. Portia gives him the chance to accept Bassanio's offer. Shylock seeks only justice. He is then defeated, for he must take the exact weight of flesh – no more and no less – and is unable to shed blood. The punishment for a foreigner taking a Venetian's life is death, and for one seeking a Venetian's life half his property goes to the state, the other half to his victim. Shylock's life is spared. Antonio proposes a settlement upon Jessica and Lorenzo of Shylock's estate, and that he administer the other half until Shylock's death, when the money will go to them. Antonio insists upon Shylock's conversion to Christianity. Shylock agrees but, feeling unwell, leaves.

The fifth section focusses upon Portia (in disguise), Antonio and Bassanio. She refuses a reward; they insist on one. Antonio persuades Bassanio to give her the ring she has asked for although he has sworn (to Portia) not to part with it.

Commentary

The five-fold structural division draws attention to the themes in the play of justice, law, mercy, religion, authority, power, judgement, reward and disguise. As ruler of Venice, the Duke presides over four of the five sequences. The conflict between Shylock, Antonio, Bassanio and Portia, and the court, concerns the nature of justice. Is the letter of the law enacted or is mercy shown? This question is reinforced at the end of the scene when Bassanio's promise to Portia (over the ring) is put aside out of consideration for the spirit of the young lawyer's behaviour.

The structure reflects character and character relationships. Antonio is well established in Venice, close to the Duke. The extent of Antonio's sacrifice for Bassanio is made evident, as is Bassanio's feeling for him. Antonio's resignation contrasts with Bassanio's anger, his mercy with Gratiano's taunting of Shylock and cries for vengeance. Shylock's insistence upon what is due to him reflects his awareness that his security depends upon the state's protection, whilst his hatred of Antonio reflects personal and social envy. A disguised Portia exhibits powerful rhetoric, high intelligence, and at the end of the scene, witty innuendo. In the fifth section a complex triangular relationship between the disguised Portia, Antonio and Bassanio emerges. Portia (as Balthazar) accepts her own ring from a Bassanio urged by Antonio to give the young lawyer recompense for his services.

The scene is one of dramatic power in the setting, situation, and characterization, with the conflict between Shylock, Venice and its representatives. The use of disguise highlights dramatic and verbal irony: all are unaware that the bright young lawyer is in fact Portia. Many elements are at work in this complex, brilliant scene amongst which word play and punning, for instance, on 'heart', 'bond', 'fair', 'gentle', and 'blood', should not be ignored.

qualify Soften.

Out of his . . . reach Away from his malice.

leadest this fashion . . . hour of act Continue your show of malice until the very last.

loose Give up.

moiety Part.

Turks, and Tartars Used by the Elizabethans as representatives of ruthlessness and cruelty.

offices of tender courtesy Merciful behaviour.

possess'd Explained to.

If you deny it . . . freedom If you don't uphold the law then Venice's freedoms will disappear. This is Shylock's trump card, as Salerio and Antonio have already realized (Act III, Scenes 2 and 3).

carrion flesh See note p.40.

is it answer'd? Notice that in reply to the Duke's request for 'a gentle answer', Shylock repeats 'answer' five times in his reply.

ban'd Destroyed.

love not a gaping pig! (a) a pig's head served at table with its mouth open (b) a squealing pig. Remember that pork is un-Kosher. Shylock couldn't eat it.

sings i'th'nose . . . their urine Another unpleasant image: when they hear a bag-pipe play this makes them urinate.

As to offend himself being offended Being himself offended must therefore offend others.

losing suit On a loser. Shylock will lose his money for the sake of worthless flesh.

current Flow, a metaphor from the movement of water or the sea.

Every offence i.e. offence taken.

bate Reduce.

bleak (a) sigh (b) bleat.

fretten Blown to and fro.

draw Take.

dearly bought Paid a high price for (Shylock has sacrificed his 3,000 ducats). Also, paid for at a high emotional cost.

tainted wether of the flock (a) the diseased ram (b) a reference to the sheep chosen to be sacrificed.

Meetest (a) fittest (b) a pun: meat.

thy sole: but on thy soul 'Sole' refers to the self, to the soul, and to being alone, so the line puns on the same sound but different meanings of the word.

metal Another pun: (a) intelligence, awareness (b) the material.

bear (a) extract (b) reveal.

pierce Another pun: (a) get through to you (b) cut you.

wit i.e. high intelligence.

inexecrable dog! i.e. one who cannot be insulted and cursed enough.

for thy life let ... accus'd (a) justice is at fault if it allows you to go on living (b) let justice remove your life even if it is unjust to execute you.

To hold opinion with Pythagoras ... trunks of men The Greek philosopher Pythagoras believed in (a) the transmigration of souls (b) the movement of animal souls into human bodies ('trunks').

fell Cruel.

unhallowed dam Non-Christian mother.

Infus'd itself in thee i.e. his soul moved into yours.

rail Argue.

offend'st Injure.

Repair thy wit good youth ... ruin Come to your senses or you'll destroy yourself.

be no impediment to let him ... estimation i.e. his youth shouldn't detract from his wisdom.

publish his commendation Reveal to everyone his excellent abilities.

Cannot impugn you as you do proceed Cannot find fault with your procedure.

his danger His power.

confess the bond Admit to making such an agreement.

be merciful (a) by nature be merciful (b) show mercy. This line is addressed to Antonio as well as to Shylock.

It droppeth as the ... place beneath Cf. Ecclesiasticus, 35,20: 'Mercy is seasonable in time of affliction as clouds of rain in the time of drought.'

mightiest in the mightiest i.e. mercy is greatest in those who have supreme power.

seasons Moderates.

that same prayer i.e. the Lord's prayer.

mitigate Moderate.

malice bears down truth Hatred triumphs over truth.

To do a great right ... little wrong To do right, the law must be flexible.

Daniel Not a reference to Daniel in the lion's den but to Daniel the youthful judge in *The Story of Susannah and the Elders* in the *Apocrypha*. During skilful cross-examination Daniel demonstrates that Susannah, who has been falsely accused and condemned by two Elders, is innocent. Portia resembles Daniel in youth and skills.

tenour Terms.

heartily Antonio, tired of waiting, wants to get the punishment over and done with. Notice the pun (a) full of agreement (b) the heart.

nominated Written.

ling'ring penance Long drawn out punishment.

process Manner.

speak me fair i.e. speak well of me. Notice that 'fair' is ironic, it can mean (a) beauty (b) correct, just (c) noble.

bid her be judge Notice the dramatic irony: in this instance Antonio doesn't know that he is indeed speaking to Portia i.e. 'her' (the audience is party to this fact, the character on stage is not).

as dear to me As (a) close to me (b) expensive or costly (c) as precious.

Your wife . . . to make the offer Ironic, Portia is indeed present.

'Tis well . . . house Again ironic. Gratiano isn't aware that he is also speaking to Nerissa, his wife.

These be the . . . daughter For a moment Shylock seems to forget that his daughter has left him. Possibly he was going to say that he wouldn't sacrifice his daughter in this way!

Barrabas Several references here. (a) to the robber released by Pilate instead of Jesus (b) to the tragic villain-hero in Christopher Marlowe's play *The Jew of Malta*.

trifle time Waste time.

'a pound of flesh' The modern metric equivalent would be about 0.454 kilograms. A 'pound' was a basic unit of weight.

Soft! Be careful! (don't forget that it's Portia's money Bassanio is offering).

a just pound (a) exactly a pound in weight (b) the correct portion or amount. Antonio's flesh has become a commercial commodity.

Or the division . . . of one poor scruple 'Scruple' has at least three meanings: (a) a moral or ethical consideration stopping one from taking a certain course of action (b) the exact amount (c) a unit of weight being, in the metric system, 1.296 grams.

But in . . . a hair Even differs by the weight of a single hair. Portia insists on the precise amount.

on the hip Again Gratiano imitates words Shylock has previously used. See Act I, Scene 3: 'If I can catch him once upon the hip.'

principal The exact amount owed, as opposed to three times the amount.

barely Merely, only.

privy coffer The private treasury.

humbleness may drive unto a fine i.e. if you are humble and ask for mercy you'll get away with a fine.

Ay for the state . . . for Antonio i.e. the state will collect the money, not Antonio.

A halter gratis A free hangman's rope.

To quit . . . his daughter Antonio asks (a) that the state exacts nothing (b) he be allowed to keep the other half of Shylock's estate in trust for Lorenzo and Jessica (c) that Shylock immediately becomes a Christian (d) that Shylock formally draws up a will leaving the half he keeps to Lorenzo and Jessica.

recant Withdraw.

I pray . . . I will sign it Shylock's final words.

gratify Reward.

much bound to him Notice several meanings: (a) connected (b) entrapped (c) beholden (c) thankful (d) the sound echoes 'bond'.

worthy Again several meanings: (a) distinguished (b) wealthy (c) excellent (d) morally upright.

in lieu whereof In return for which.

freely cope i.e. give you without hesitation – the money is Portia's.

And I delivering . . . mercenary i.e. only wished to do what was right rather than directed by financial or other considerations of gain.

you know me . . . meet again Note the irony: the words are addressed to her husband. Portia hopes that he'll recognize her (remember she is disguised as a young man).

of force . . . you further Feel necessary to try again to persuade you.

press me far You push me hard.

I'll take this ring from you She knows exactly what to ask for. It is a gift Bassanio will not willingly part with. The ring is a symbol of unity, mutual possession, their love, fidelity to each other – i.e. Bassanio and Portia (Nerissa and Gratiano). Remember too that the loss of his wife's ring had deeply disturbed Shylock.

it is a trifle . . . you this! Bassanio claims that the ring is insignificant, unaware that he is addressing Portia.

The dearest ring (a) the most expensive (b) underlying meaning of most precious in an emotional sense.

first to beg To ask for a reward.

That scuse serves many men Portia is speaking about herself. Bassanio of course is unaware of this. Her lines are an excellent illustration of (a) verbal irony (the implicit meaning intended by the speaker differs from that which she seems to assert) (b) dramatic irony.

She would not hold out . . . for ever Notice that literally this is true. Portia's 'anger' soon disappears at the end of the play.

Let his deservings . . . wife's commandment i.e. value what he deserves and my love for you above your wife's orders. Again ironic, because a disguised Portia has asked for the ring.

Act IV Scene 2

Portia instructs Nerissa to find Shylock's house and give him the new will to sign. Overtaking Portia (still disguised as Balthazar),

Gratiano gives her Bassanio's ring, repeats the dinner invitation, and agrees to show Nerissa Shylock's house. In an aside, Nerissa tells Portia that she too will try to get Bassanio to give up his ring in order to play a joke on him. Portia takes great delight in playing the double ring joke on their husbands and considers what excuses their men will make.

Commentary

This short scene with its joke about the exchanging of the rings is in obvious contrast to the previous lengthy trial scene. It emerges directly from the preoccupation with rings evident at the end of the last scene. Note the word-play, the way in which the scene emphasizes the themes in the play of appearance and reality, trust and deceit – Portia and Nerissa are still disguised – and its concerns with fidelity, love and possessions. Portia and Nerissa obviously enjoy immensely the games they are playing. Though Shylock may have left the stage in despair, his presence is still felt.

deed i.e. revised will (as previously arranged in Act IV, Scene 1). Notice that the word is repeated in line 4 to become a pun both on the legal meaning and sense of achievement.
well Specially, very.
Fair Good.
advice Thought, reflection.
That cannot be Portia has refused the Duke's dinner invitation (Act IV, Scene 1). She can hardly accept Bassanio's invitation.
show my youth i.e. Nerissa (dressed as a male), and thus drawing attention to the consummate acting of Portia and Nerissa in their male parts.
warrant Trust, believe.
old swearing Lots of talking and pleading.
outface Challenge, brazen it out, drawing attention again to the fact that they are disguised as males.

Revision questions on Act IV

1 Write an account of the trial scene, bringing out its dramatic qualities.
2 Whom do you consider to be the central figure in the trial scene? Quote from the text in support of your answer.

3 Explain in some detail why it is that Shylock loses his case against Antonio.

4 Explain carefully Portia's (Balthazar's) role in the trial scene.

5 What happens after Shylock's departure in this act?

Act V Scene 1

The final scene, with its romantic moonlit setting, is in complete contrast to the earlier Venetian scenes.

As the act opens, Lorenzo and Jessica are attempting to outdo each other with references to famous mythical lovers who on such a night were faithful and unfaithful. They are interrupted by Portia's servant Stephano who announces his mistress's arrival, and by Launcelot Gobbo's antics. Meanwhile Lorenzo and Jessica reflect on the inner harmony and peace created by music.

Portia and Nerissa arrive, followed soon after by Bassanio, Antonio, and Gratiano. A lengthy comic episode follows in which Bassanio and Gratiano are accused of unfaithfulness to their vows by giving away Portia's and Nerissa's rings. Portia and Nerissa reveal that the rings were given to them when they were disguised, and a letter explains Portia's actions. The play's outstanding financial problems are resolved and *The Merchant of Venice* ends on Gratiano's note of bawdy punning.

Commentary

The romantic setting, references to undying romantic love, comments on the inner musical harmony of the universe, do not detract from the serious underlying issues of the play. The three pairs of lovers are at last together, the financial problems are resolved, Launcelot Gobbo has found a home; however, the irony involved in Portia's and Nerissa's elaborate, ring-joke deception, focusses attention on some of the play's central *motifs*: deceit; illusion; fidelity; property; possessions; vows; bonds. Antonio's pledge once again to help Bassanio, this time with his soul rather than his flesh, serves also as a timely reminder of the Shylock part of the play. Notice that ironically at the end of the play Antonio remains alone on stage without a partner.

The moon . . . make no noise Fine example of onomatopoeia: the 'o', 't' and 's' sounds resemble the sound of the wind.

Troilus . . . Trojan . . . Cressid Troilus, son of the King of Troy, and Cressid were lovers and had exchanged vows of eternal fidelity. However, during the siege of Troy, Cressid was handed over to the Greeks in an exchange of prisoners. She vowed to remain constant but soon fell in love with Diomed. For a long time, every night Troilus stood on the walls of Troy looking at the Greek camp. Chaucer in his poem *Troilus and Cresseyde* told the story and Cressid became a symbol for unfaithful lovers. Shakespeare also based a play on the story *Troilus and Cressida*.

In such a night Notice that these words are repeated eight times during Lorenzo's and Jessica's reflections on great sad romances, and convey a sense of fate and destiny. The use of 'In', rather than 'On', implies both on and during such a night, thereby drawing attention to the romantic sentimental associations of moonlight and love.

Thisbe A Babylonian legend used by Shakespeare in *A Midsummer Night's Dream*, by Chaucer in *Legend of Good Women*, and by the Roman poet Ovid. Forbidden by their parents to meet, Pyramus and Thisbe had to arrange secret meetings. Thisbe, whilst waiting for Pyramus, was frightened by a lion and fled, leaving behind her cloak, which was mauled by the lion. Seeing her blood-stained cloak Pyramus, thinking Thisbe dead, killed himself. Thisbe returned, saw her beloved's body, and killed herself too. Both came to represent faithful lovers.

lion's shadow ere himself i.e. the lion's shadow was reflected before Thisbe actually saw it.

Dido . . . Carthage In the Roman poet Virgil's *Aeneid*, Dido, the Queen of Carthage, a marvellous city of the ancient world located in North Africa, falls in love with Aeneas, the founder of Rome. He was forced to leave her and to sail away. When he left she burnt herself to death.

Stood Dido . . . Carthage Another example of onomatopoeia: the 'o', 'w' sounds echoing Dido's sadness.

willow A symbol of unrequited love and sadness.

waft Waved to (in the past).

Medea . . . Æson Æson's youth was restored by Medea, the wife of his son, Jason: this was done by gathering herbs at full moon. Jason, however, was an unfaithful husband and Medea poisoned his children. The story is told by Ovid. The reference to the restoration of youth suggests that Jessica is hinting to Lorenzo that he is a rather slow lover. See also Act I, Scene 1, the note on 'Colchos' and 'Jasons'.

unthrift Poor – i.e. Lorenzo himself.

did run from An allusion to all of the previously mentioned legendary figures who also ran away.

Stealing (a) the word echoes Lorenzo's 'steal' (b) Jessica has taken and removed her father's jewels. (c) Lorenzo has taken Jessica and her religion from her (d) to obtain.

I would out-night Go one better than you in recounting things which happened 'in such a night'.

holy crosses Roadside crosses are common in France, Italy and other Catholic countries.

my master i.e. Bassanio.

Sola . . . sola! Launcelot imitates the sound of the huntsman's post-horn – in itself a symbol of masculine virility and a humorous contrast to the witty cross-talk of Jessica and Lorenzo.

horn (a) the instrument announcing the post's arrival (b) the horn of plenty, a symbol of abundance.

touches As the fingers on the strings of the instruments.

patens (a) small golden dishes on which bread is put during the Holy Communion services. (b) metal plates (c) an image of joining together, of Communion – Lorenzo, Jessica, the harmony of music and of the world itself.

orb (a) circle (b) heavenly body.

motion like an . . . sings A reference to the idea that the earth was in the centre of a universe of hollow spheres revolving around it. The movement of the spheres created a perfect harmonic music which could not be heard by human ears. The music was that of the angels.

Still quiring to . . . cherubins Still singing as a choir to the cherubims, i.e. kinds of angels close to God. The cherubims with their child-like features are the emblems of God's closeness to humans and, according to tradition, they aid those in distress. So literally the orbs sing continuously to the ever-young cherubims thus conveying the idea of everlasting youth and harmony, and the ability to appreciate harmony.

this muddy vesture of decay i.e. human life, the body. Another reference to the transitory nature of human life contrasted with the eternal life of the universe.

grossly close it in i.e. enclosed in our decaying human bodies we cannot hear the everlasting music of the heavens.

Diana The moon Goddess. See note Act I, Scene 2.

spirits are attentive (The) mind is elsewhere, (you) aren't concentrating on the music.

unhandled Unbroken, untrained.

Fetching . . . loud Making lots of noise. Note the lengthy line and onomatopoeic effects with 'b' sounds and the monosyllabic 'loud' at the end of the line which convey the sense of chaos and anarchy. Lorenzo expresses a frenzied dream.

turn'd to a modest gaze Toned down, moderated. Lorenzo is saying that music will even quiet the uncontrolled and chaotic.

the poet i.e. Ovid.

Orpheus Ovid in his *Metamorphoses*, 10,11, tells the story of the great musician who went with Jason in his quest for the golden fleece and whose music had such power that the wild animals, trees, and rocks (i.e. stones) followed him in order to listen.

stockish Inanimate, hard e.g. stones (rocks), trees and floods.

stratagems and spoils Plots and violent theft. A rather startlingly horrific image from Lorenzo.

motions Impulses.

Erebus In classical mythology the home of the dead, an area of darkness near Hell.

How far that . . . beams! Note the metaphor; a small candle becomes transformed into a symbol of goodness. Literally, a candle doesn't have beams, the moon does. So 'his' refers to the moon – an idea taken up by Nerissa.

So shines a . . . world The world and good deeds are personified, transformed into people and human behaviour.

So doth . . . the less Again notice that the meaning focusses on the contrast between appearance and reality, the real and the superficial.

Nothing is good . . . respect Things are relative.

Methinks . . . by day Music played at night sounds sweeter than during the day.

How many things by season . . . perfection! i.e. at the right time many things are praised and correctly appreciated as they should be. There is a pun on 'season, season'd': (a) the time (b) ripe, ready (c) of wood in musical instruments which are ready for playing and producing the most resonant sound (d) as used in 'seasoning' food.

Peace! . . . Endymion Endymion in classical mythology was a handsome boy. Selene, the moon-goddess, fell in love with him, kissed him, and caused him to sleep for ever so that every night she could be with him. Portia stops the musicians playing and probably draws attention to Lorenzo and Jessica – a pair of 'mooning' lovers.

speed (a) improves (b) hurries back to us.

for our words A reference to the activities at the end of the last act – the exchange of rings.

We should hold day with . . . absence of the sun An elaborate compliment. If Portia walks at night she will illuminate it as the sun does the other side of the world. When we are in darkness, the other side is in daylight.

give light . . . be light Punning, meaning provide pleasure – but not be unfaithful. See also Act II, Scene 6 where the word is used with similar implications.

God sort all God resolves everything.

infinitely bound (a) in debt to (b) connected in friendship.

in all sense . . . bound for you i.e. in every respect. Notice the punning on the repeated word 'bound'. In addition to the meanings used by Bassanio, Portia's comment also refers to Antonio's love for Bassanio, his imprisonment on his behalf, and his going into 'bondage' for him.

acquitted of Released from.

I scant this breathing courtesy i.e. I stop this merely formal welcome.

gelt Castrated.

posy Poetry – the ring was engraved with an inscription.

respective Careful. Remember this is all irony. The audience, Portia and Nerissa know exactly what has happened.

scrubbed boy i.e. short boy. Gratiano is adding insult to injury, for Nerissa herself is the 'scrubbed boy'!

No higher than thyself This is ironic because it is literally true.

prating Gossiping.

for my heart (a) in my heart (b) for your sake.

masters Possesses. A startling image implying that the ring meant more than all the wealth of the world. In a sense, to Portia it does.

If you did know The repetition in these lines gives force to what Bassanio says.

ring Bassanio repeats the word five times, as does Portia. The word does indeed 'ring'!

virtue (a) power (b) real significance.

wanted the modesty ... a ceremony So lacking in manners as to insist upon the ring which was regarded as a sacred emblem.

civil doctor A doctor of civil law.

besmear it Discredit it.

the jewel that I loved Note again the connection between material value and human feeling which echoes throughout the play. Notice also that Portia uses the word 'loved' in the past tense. She clearly enjoys torturing Bassanio.

liberal (a) free (b) generous with property and affections – in the sexual sense.

Argus In classical mythology, a person with a hundred eyes.

well advis'd Pay much attention.

pen (a) writing instrument (b) penis.

enforced Unavoidable.

doubly Ironic pun – (a) he sees Portia (b) he sees the lawyer to whom he gave the ring (c) to physically 'double up'.

of credit (a) of truth (b) of financial backing.

wealth Welfare. However the financial meaning is also implicit.

My soul upon the forfeit Again Antonio offers himself for Bassanio – this time his soul i.e. his spirit rather than his flesh.

advisedly Deliberately.

it i.e. the ring.

I had it ... lay with me Notice the irony and implications: (a) she was the doctor (b) she received the ring (c) the ring was with her.

gentle Gratiano ... scrubbed boy This time Nerissa repeats Gratiano's words, another example of her humour.

cuckolds Husbands whose wives have been unfaithful.

grossly (a) ignorantly (b) in a coarse manner.

a letter The loose ends are tied up. The letter clarifies the outstanding issues of Antonio's wealth and Portia's disguise.

I knew you not I didn't recognize you.

manna Exodus 16,14–36. The food miraculously supplied to the
Israelites wandering in the desert.

charge us there . . . inter'gatories (a) ask questions to be answered on
oath (b) sexually make us aware, i.e. answer our questions as women.

couching (a) lying with (b) having intercourse with.

ring A final ringing pun! (a) the actual ring (b) Nerissa's sexual organs.

Revision questions on Act V

1 In what ways does this act provide a contrast to the trial scene
in Act IV?

2 Discuss the significance of 'rings' in this act.

3 How is the atmosphere of Belmont created? (You should
refer to the action, the setting, the dialogue, the imagery.)

4 In what ways do you consider that this act provides a fitting
conclusion to the play? Give reasons for your answer, and refer
closely to the text.

5 Say in what ways you find this act (a) humorous and (b)
romantic.

General questions

Note style answer

1 How are the main plots related to the sub-plots in *The Merchant of Venice*?

Two main plots: (a) the bond story; (b) the casket story.
Two sub-plots: (a) the Lorenzo-Jessica plot; (b) the ring plot.

These interweave through use of (a) similar sets of characters (b) similar and contrasting settings (c) similar kinds of meaning (d) the same imagery.

Bassanio initiates main plot – needs money to court Portia. Antonio offers money and help, takes additional loans from Shylock. Bond agreement – failure to repay Shylock – rescued by Portia in disguise. Portia – rich heiress – is courted by various suitors who must 'give and hazard all' (Act II, Scene 7) – choice of casket. Bassanio makes right choice. Tells Portia Antonio in debt. He must return to Venice.

Shylock insists upon pound of flesh. After trial scene, Bassanio insists that Portia-Balthazar be rewarded – insists upon ring. Bassanio unable to penetrate Portia's disguise. Shylock reacts to loss of turquoise – its emotional value is high. The ring a link with past, love, fidelity.

All characters ringed in by the sea, in Portia's case by father's will. Final word of play 'ring': for a woman Antonio's life placed in danger, Shylock angered and banished. Jessica betrays father for a man. The word 'ring' unites the main plots (the bond and the casket) with the sub-plots (Jessica, the rings).

1 How are the main plots related to the sub-plots in *The Merchant of Venice*?
2 Which main images occur throughout the play and what is their significance?
3 What are the dominant themes of the play?
4 Write an essay on word-play in *The Merchant of Venice*.
5 What is the significance of the casket scenes?

6 Discuss the relationship in the play between the Belmont and Venetian settings and characterization.

7 Compare and contrast the characters of Antonio and Shylock: why are they enemies?

8 Write an essay on the character and role in the play of *one* of the following: (a) Jessica (b) Lorenzo (c) Nerissa and Gratiano (d) Salerio and Solanio.

9 Describe the use in the play of words with double meanings.

10 '*The Merchant of Venice* is a play about friendship.' Discuss.

11 What is the role of Bassanio in the play?

12 Which aspects of Portia's character are revealed (a) when she reviews her suitors (b) when she hears of Antonio's arrest (c) at Shylock's trial (d) in the last act of the play?

13 Discuss the role of the sea and ships in the play.

14 'Shylock is more sinned against than sinning.' Discuss.

15 Consider the role and function of Launcelot Gobbo in the play.

16 Why are 'bonds' so important in the play?

17 Discuss the role of play-acting and disguise in *The Merchant of Venice*.

18 Assess the function of classical allusions in *The Merchant of Venice*.

19 Discuss the importance of rings and jewelry in the play.

20 Do you think that *The Merchant of Venice* is an appropriate title for the play?

21 Describe the love relationships in the play.

22 '*The Merchant of Venice* is a twin study of loneliness' (Midgley) – Shylock's and Antonio's. Discuss.

23 Discuss the part irony and dramatic irony play in *The Merchant of Venice*.

24 'Omit Antonio and Shylock and the play becomes a romantic fairy tale like *A Midsummer's Night's Dream*' (W. H. Auden). Discuss.

25 What role does music play in *The Merchant of Venice*?

Shakespeare's art in
The Merchant of Venice
Setting

The great majority of Shakespeare's plays, apart from the English Histories, are set in places abroad, a device which of itself gave them a romantic colouring.

The local colour of all Shakespeare's plays is that of Elizabethan England, whether the story is one of Italy, Denmark or Scotland and in whatever age. Here Shakespeare's drama is set in Venice, at the time an influential city, a cultural and trading crossroads between the East and the West. It was a great seaport, a point of contact and of collision between Catholicism and Protestantism, North Western Europeans, Greeks, Italians, many varieties of Christians and differing kinds of Jews. This last group lived largely in the ghetto area, crowded in a small area of the city. They came from many different countries and were primarily engaged in trade and shipping. A way out of the narrow confines of the ghetto was through conversion, a path Jessica chooses to follow. A baptized Jew was legally allowed to receive money. The Jewish ghetto was a cramped hive of activity. Jessica's marriage to Lorenzo affords her the opportunity of gaining access to the restful and relaxed Belmont across the waters.

Note how in *The Merchant of Venice* Shakespeare has paid more attention to accurate local colour than is usual with him. The carrying-trade of Venice between East and West ('the trade and profit of the city consisteth of all nations') is continually brought home to us, and we are made to realize the city's place among the waters by Bassanio's voyage to Belmont and Portia's in the other direction on 'the tranect', 'the common ferry which trades to Venice'. The Doge himself appears in the play, the rich merchants meet on the Rialto (IV,1), where the chief topic of conversation is the news of their argosies at sea (I,3, and III,1), Lorenzo and Jessica escape in a gondola (II,8), and Old Gobbo brings a present of a dish of doves for Bassanio (II,2). But by far the most realistic touch is speaking of England as if it were a foreign country (I,2, II,8, III,1), especially the last of these, with its casual and dramatic 'the Goodwins, *I think they call the place*'.

The characters

Shylock

I hate him for he is a Christian:
But more, for that in low simplicity
He lends out money gratis, and brings down
The rate of usance here with us in Venice.
If I can catch him once upon the hip,
I will feed fat the ancient grudge I bear him.

(I,3)

The character of Shylock has spawned an enormous amount of literature. Critics have focussed largely upon three issues: the ways in which Shylock has been performed on the stage through the centuries; whether Shylock is simply a malevolent, nasty, revengeful Jew demanding what he feels he deserves and showing no mercy to his victims; or whether Shakespeare's portrait of Shylock is more rounded and complex.

In Act III, Scene 1 Shylock is given powerful prose. He asks the merchant Salerio

Hath not a Jew eyes? hath not a Jew hands, organs, dimensions, senses, affections, passions? fed with the same food, hurt with the same weapons, subject to the same diseases, healed by the same means, warmed and cooled by the same winter and summer as a Christian is? – if you prick us do we not bleed? if you tickle us do we not laugh? if you poison us do we not die? and if you wrong us shall we not revenge?

Sentiments common to humanity are conveyed through the use of repeated rhetorical questions 'Hath not a Jew . . .', repetitive monosyllables which assert basic points and which together create a powerful cumulative effect. Notice that the categories are divided into the physical – 'hands', 'organs' – and the psychological – 'sense', 'affections', 'passions'. Further elements in this magnificent passage are the contrast between the seasons 'winter and summer', natural disease, recovery processes, healing and the natural things all of us are subject to: pricking, bleeding, tickling, laughing, poisoning, dying, wronging and revenging.

In many ways, then, Shylock is the representative of us all. But the origins of his name indicate his role and the interpretative problems which are raised by his personality and presence. His name is an obscure one. If the two syllables in it are separated interesting elements emerge. 'Shy' fits two Hebrew names: Saul the name of the King before the famous King David; 'seol' which in Hebrew is associated with death and the underworld. In addition there is a Hebrew root verb 'sal' meaning to lend or borrow. Lending is crucial to the plot of *The Merchant of Venice*: traditionally it is a means by which the Devil lures men into his trap.

If Shylock is the representative of us all, then what are our, what are his, redeeming features? They are that he feels and suffers just as we do. But he is a member of a race against which there is prejudice. A very deep residue of anti-Jewish sentiment would inevitably have been present in Shakespeare's audience, a prejudice fuelled by injunctions against usury and dramatic depictions of evil Jews such as Marlowe's *The Jew of Malta*.

Shylock does not dominate every scene of *The Merchant of Venice*. He is actually on stage only in Act I Scene 3, Act II Scene 5, Act III Scenes 1 and 3 and finally in the classic trial scene, Act IV Scene 1. He is referred to (for instance, by Launcelot Gobbo in Act II Scene 2) when not on stage. In Act II Scene 3 Jessica bitterly regrets being his daughter 'Alack, what heinous sin is it in me' she confesses 'To be ashamed to be my father's child.' Shylock's brooding presence is felt long after he has left the stage.

Socially Shylock is needed in Venice. There has to be a money-lender. Antonio has to borrow from someone and it is Shylock to whom he turns. Shylock's first words in the play 'Three thousand ducats, well' serve to emphasize his financial role. He plays the numbers game. Indeed it is difficult to distinguish the real Shylock from his social role. Act I, Scene 3 contains a crucial dramatic conflict in the play. Although the confrontation between Antonio and Shylock is prefaced by the less hostile meeting between Bassanio and Shylock, the subject is the same: money, interest and Antonio's credit rating – i.e. can Antonio repay his debts? Remember that although money-lending was crucial to Venetian society, Christianity frowned upon it. The job of lending money was left to the Jews, who were despised for performing a necessary social task. For Shylock there can be no socializing between himself, Bassanio and Antonio. Their meetings are professional only, and Shylock treats Antonio and Bassanio with the same contempt that they have for him. Shylock tells Bassanio: 'I will buy with you, sell with you, talk with you, walk with you, and so following: but I will not eat with you, drink with you, nor pray with you.' Shylock is as prejudiced as his enemies.

Antonio and Bassanio are dwarfed intellectually by Shylock whose attitudes are largely formed by Biblical interpretation. His use of the story of Laban's sheep in Act I, Scene 3 is a marvellous example of his intellectual skill. For Shylock the creation of money is creative. He is proud to make money 'breed as fast' as rams and ewes. He considers 'well won thrift' what Antonio refers to negatively as 'interest'. Shylock appears to be a calculating, ruthless businessman. Much of what he does is generated by emotional reactions to the social role he is forced to play. His is a different system of values. Shylock has nothing but contempt for Antonio. When he first sees him he scornfully comments 'How like a fawning publican he looks!' Business rivalry, contrasted attitudes to the way business is conducted and fierce national and religious loyalty are interwoven in his reactions to Antonio. Emotionally Shylock is unable to withstand the daily humiliations he is subjected to by Antonio and his companions. Associating his personal situation with the history of his people, Shylock cries out 'Sufferance is the badge of all my tribe.' Shylock's characteristic speech pattern is to ask questions which sometimes he answers himself and sometimes not. At times he quotes the Old Testament, directly addresses God, and speaks to others without expecting an answer. Antonio and Shylock rarely talk to each other: they address unseen witnesses.

Shylock's Achilles heel is his daughter Jessica. She reacts against the harsh regimentation to which she has been subjected, being told, for instance, in Act II, Scene 5 not to 'thrust' her 'head into the public street/To gaze on Christian fools'. Shylock trusts her with his house, his property and his keys. Solanio in Act II, Scene 8 recounts Shylock's outraged and deranged reaction at Jessica's behaviour:

I never heard a passion so confus'd,
So strange, outrageous, and so variable
As the dog Jew did utter in the streets, –
'My daughter! O my ducats! O my daughter
Fled with a Christian! O my Christian ducats!'

Shylock's love and trust have been violated and he feels humiliated. Emotions of fatherly love for a single daughter are mixed with feelings of shame, loss and betrayal. Shylock's reactions are not without irony. Literally, Jessica is his treasure. His reactions seem to focus more upon the loss of a valuable turquoise ring than upon the loss of his daughter. The ring has associations with Leah, his dead wife. Shylock's comment 'I would not have given it away for a wilderness of monkeys' demonstrates that there are for him values above and beyond the financial. The ring has a much, perhaps even more, symbolic, associational and sentimental value for him as have the rings Portia and Nerissa verbally duel over with Bassanio and Gratiano in the last Act. The loss for Shylock is especially bitter, for the ring has been removed by his daughter – his 'flesh and blood'. It is this loss and bitterness which provide the fuel for his insistence upon revenge, and which help bring about Shylock's downfall.

Shylock is obsessed with revenge, has Antonio imprisoned and will not listen to requests for reason. He tells Antonio

'I'll have my bond, speak not against my bond
I have sworn on oath, that I will have my bond.'

It is as if Shylock intends to replace his daughter's lost flesh with Antonio's flesh. In the trial scene Shylock's sincerity, passion, consistency and unstoppable desire for revenge, his refusal to forgive, counterpoint the pomp and ceremony of the setting in the grand Venetian court of justice with the Duke, the supreme ruler and 'Magnificoes' allied against him. Shylock the outsider demanding what he feels is right is pitted against the might, the structures of Venetian power. This scene can be played theatrically for all that it is worth. There is considerable dramatic suspense. Shylock prepares the knife for 'a pound of carrion flesh'. He is destroyed at the eleventh hour by a piece of legal trickery carried out by a young girl disguised as a lawyer. He leaves the stage alone and frustrated with the words 'I am not well.' His spirit hovers over the rest of the drama. It places the Belmont revels of the last act in perspective, emphasizing that in life amidst happiness there is great sadness and isolation.

To sum up then, Shylock presents interpretative problems. The chief of these is to distinguish if possible between his role as representative of an ethnic group more sinned against than sinning, and his behaviour as a human being. Shylock pleads in his great speech 'Hath not a Jew eyes?' for judgement as a person and not as a racial stereotype. He can be vicious, cunning, avaricious, cruel and heartless. He is without a friend (even Tubal seems to take a malicious delight in 'torturing' him), without a soul to speak a good word for him, and the boys of Venice mock him in the streets; yet a pathos clings about him to the end. Shakespeare exhibits the ordinary Elizabethan prejudice against the Jew. Other people's attitudes to Shylock have partly made him what he is: intelligent, resourceful, the practitioner of a trade Christians scorn, nationally proud, religious, a tough father. Shylock is a proud sensitive man bitterly hurt by his daughter's actions with whom we as human beings cannot help but sympathize. Shakespeare makes us see Shylock not only as the other characters see him, but as he sees himself. This vision and insight make the character of Shylock what it is.

Portia

In Belmont is a lady richly left,
And she is fair, and (fairer than that word),
Of wondrous virtues

Such is Bassanio's assessment of Portia's worth at the beginning of the play. Portia is 'a lady richly left' – in other words, she is very wealthy. She retains enormous power and influence over her possessions and estates until the correct casket choice is made. Portia is 'fair' financially, physically and psychologically. She is the recipient of classical comparisons and indeed her name alludes to her bravery, wisdom, learning and love for her husband. Bassanio tells Antonio:

Nor is the wide world ignorant of her worth,
For the four winds blow in from every coast
Renowned suitors, and her sunny locks
Hang on her temples like a gold fleece
Which makes her seat of Belmont Colchos' strond
And many Jasons come in quest of her.

Portia is a rich prize, to be coveted, won and possessed. She has become as the 'golden fleece' of classical legend – the object of desire and quests.

Portia serves dramatically not only as a physical and intellectual contrast to the dark, older Shylock. The world she controls, Belmont with its gardens and ornate setting, directly contrasts with the narrow Venetian streets and squares in which business is transacted. Portia represents inherited wealth which can be obtained through marriage and a gamble with casket choice. She contrasts with the wealth of Venice, a product of trade and shipping and at the mercy of nature. Portia is at the mercy of choice. The Venetian merchants are at the mercy of the sea and its mercurial temperament. Portia is trapped not by the sea and ships but by the restrictions of her father's will. Like Antonio in the first scene of the play, she too is depressed and also has to be comforted by a friend. Her first line indicates the unfulfilled element in her personality: 'By my troth Nerissa, my little body is aweary of this great world.'

Nerissa draws Portia's attention to the difference between her psychological state of mind and her financial position, telling her that she would be unhappy 'if' her 'miseries were in the same abundance as' her 'good fortunes are'. Portia is the major focus of the casket scenes which are primarily preoccupied with the division between appearance and reality, allusion, and the theme of intrinsic value as contrasted with external glitter. Portia's suitors must choose from three caskets of gold, silver and lead. It is the lead casket which contains Portia's portrait and not the superficially more attractive gold and silver caskets. She, however, must wait comparatively helpless, watching her fate being decided.

Portia has social bearing and good breeding. On the whole she is able to behave with dignity whilst being inspected by, at times, arrogant suitors in the manner of a highly-priced racehorse. Her comments on these suitors are confined to asides to Nerissa rather than in public comments which would abuse the rules of hospitality. In Act I, Scene 2 she waits till the suitors have left before making witty, caustic observations at their expense. Portia is able to separate public and private duties. She adapts herself to changes in mood and temperament and is aware just how suitors such as Morocco and Arragon would mistreat her. She is loyal and dutiful to the terms of her father's will, although her private bias and preference reveals itself when Bassanio appears as a suitor. Through the use of subtle verbal innuendo and body language she probably helps him make the correct choice.

Portia's intelligence is exhibited when she elects to marry Bassanio as soon as he has made his choice. She then counsels him to leave at once for Venice in order to help his friend Antonio. So she is able to think and act quickly when the situation demands it. Her ingenuity shines through when, dressed up in male costume, she brilliantly acts out the role of a learned lawyer. However, her insistence on gaining Bassanio's ring as some form of payment for her legal services is a consummate form of trickery. Although this is an elaborate practical joke, she and Nerissa thoroughly enjoy tormenting Bassanio and Gratiano about their supposed unfaithfulness and lack of constancy in giving away their rings. Such deliberate enjoyment of others' discomfort exhibits an unpleasant side to Portia's character.

Her conduct during the trial scene reveals verbal rhetorical brilliance and a court-room alertness which could only come with years of experience or inherited ability. Portia reasons with Shylock to get him to relent, appeals to his mercy, to his financial sense, and then to both. She gives him many opportunities to change his mind, and even calls Antonio to speak in his own defence. When Shylock refuses to climb down, she relentlessly and remorselessly breaks him. The confrontation between the two, on the one hand the angry, elderly Shylock, and on the other the young, fair Portia disguised as a lawyer using sweet rhetoric about the 'quality of mercy', is one of the classic confrontations of the theatre. Shylock leaves the court broken and unwell. Portia, still in disguise, plays verbal games with her husband. Portia's conduct is not beyond reproach. The trial is held by her under false pretence about her identity. She is not a lawyer, or male, and is far from being a disinterested party. As Bassanio's wife it is in her interests that the debt remains unpaid, or is at least satisfactorily resolved.

Portia is skilled in dealing with people. She boosts Bassanio's talents and plays down her own. Immediately he has made the correct choice of casket she tells him 'Myself, and what is mine, to you and yours/Is now converted.' It is difficult to believe her literally when she says she 'Is an unlesson'd girl, unschool'd, unpractised' – unless she means to refer to her lack of sexual experience. Her conduct throughout the play shows her to be both wise and worldly. She is unselfish, and willingly surrenders all her property to Bassanio and offers him as much as he needs in order to save his friend Antonio. At no time does she appear jealous of Antonio or regard him as a rival for Bassanio's affections.

Her sense of humour reveals itself in comments to Nerissa

about her suitors. During the trial scene she deliberately exploits the irony of the situation when Bassanio offers to sacrifice her and her money for Antonio's life. The disguised Portia playfully comments: 'Your wife would give you little thanks for that/If she were to hear you make the offer.' The last act of the play reverberates with her repartee, puns and irony which centre upon the exchanged rings.

Antonio

I hold the world but as the world Gratiano,
A stage, where every man must play a part,
And mine a sad one.

Structurally there can be no doubt that Antonio has a crucial role in the play. Most of the action directly or indirectly concerns him. His loan from Shylock, his entering into a bond with Shylock, enable Bassanio to go to Belmont. Antonio's desire to reward the brilliant young lawyer after the trial scene provokes the ring complications. Surprisingly for a character with such a crucial structural role, Antonio is not developed and has few lines in the play. He appears in six scenes and speaks about one hundred and eighty lines.

Antonio is a merchant of power and influence. His ships travel far and wide. His wealth is dispersed and he is esteemed for his reliability. His arch-enemy Shylock comments that he is 'a good man', i.e. Antonio's bank account is sound, although Shylock realizes that Antonio's wealth is too dispersed: 'he hath squand'red abroad' (Act I, Scene 3). According to Bassanio, Antonio is

'one in whom
The ancient Roman honour more appears
Than any that draws breath in Italy' (III,2).

The Duke of Venice, his 'magnificoes', have tried in vain to persuade Shylock not to insist upon his bond. In prison Antonio is given special privileges. The respect he is held in is not due to his wealth, for his friends remain with him after he has suffered a reverse in fortune. Antonio's innate kindness and noble qualities impress everyone. Salerio says that 'A kinder gentleman treads not on the earth.' Part of Shylock's hatred for Antonio lies in the fact that Antonio has lent out money without interest, has helped debtors and is generally ready to assist people in trouble.

Altruism, however, is not the reason why Antonio tells Bassanio 'My purse, my person, my extremest means/Lie all unlock'd to your occasions' (Act I, Scene 1). Salerio, in his account of Antonio's departure from Bassanio, relates the grief at parting. Antonio 'wrung Bassanio's hand' and Salerio comments 'I think he only loves the world for him.' Antonio, emotionally and physically, is obsessed with Bassanio and in order to please him is prepared to sacrifice both his fortune and his life.

The sad, melancholic, self-absorbed, element in Antonio is evident from his opening line: 'In sooth I know not why I am so sad'. Indeed the opening section of the play is taken up with the efforts of his friends to cheer him up and to find the reasons for his unhappiness. Throughout the play Antonio is muted, unhappy and frustrated. And at the close of the play, Antonio, his wealth restored, surrounded by friends is again 'dumb', bereft of words and real sustaining comfort. He is left alone whilst the couples Portia and Bassanio, Nerissa and Gratiano, Jessica and Lorenzo, go their separate ways.

The duality in Antonio between external appearances and internal realities is reflected in his language. He tells Gratiano in the opening scene 'I hold the world but as the world . . ./A stage, where every man must play a part,/And mine a sad one.' Words frequently used by him are 'worth', 'dear' and 'fortune' which emphasize both financial and emotional meaning. Antonio's sadness is partly an awareness of the thin borderline between social respect based upon wealth and social isolation based upon poverty. His sadness is also due to the fact that he knows that he cannot have that which he most desires – Bassanio. Antonio is a gambler. He knows the hazards of his trade and is aware of the perils of the oceans.

An emotional outlet for Antonio is his intense hatred for Shylock and for Jews. The encounter between Shylock and Antonio in Act I, Scene 3 shows the deep religious, ideological and personal differences between the two. Antonio professes that he neither 'lends nor borrows money' for gain. He is not averse, however, from taking a loan from Shylock in order to help Bassanio. For Antonio Shylock is associated with evil, he 'Is like a villain with a smiling cheek/A goodly apple rotting at the heart' (I,3), and the image of a rotting apple and heart clings to Antonio.

During the trial scene Antonio doesn't wish to argue 'with the Jew' whose 'Jewish heart' is hard. He describes himself as

'a tainted wether of the flock
Meetest for death – the weakest kind of fruit
Drops earliest to the ground, and so let me.'

These lines perhaps unconsciously echo lines spoken by Shylock to Antonio in Act I, Scene 3 when he describes Laban's sheep to him. Antonio continually puns on the word 'heart'. 'Most heartily I do beseech the court/To give the judgment' he says. He is about to pay for his 'debt' to Shylock and with his 'heart' for his love for Bassanio.

Antonio's generosity is not evenly distributed. He insists that Shylock become a Christian, and all traces of kindness on Shylock's part are attributed to the 'christian' elements in his character. Antonio's generosity emerges when he thinks of Lorenzo's and Jessica's welfare, and he retains part of Shylock's estate in trust for them. Antonio is, to conclude, crucial to the structure, imagery and meaning of the play. The conflict between Antonio and Shylock is a basic one between different religions, ways of looking at life and economic activity, and different human beings. Antonio is a gambler who stakes all, not on the choice of casket, but on fair weather at sea. He puts his 'fair flesh' at risk in order to satisfy the wishes of the man he loves who can never return his love. Antonio truly is, to cite the opening line of *The Merchant of Venice* 'so sad'.

Bassanio

Good signiors both when shall we laugh? say, when? (I,1).

Bassanio initiates the bond plot by requiring money for his Belmont venture; he connects the Venetian and Belmont worlds and places his friend Antonio within Shylock's power. More is learnt about Bassanio's virtues from others than from himself. He partly embodies Rennaissance ideals of the nobleman, courtly, handsome, and well-bred. Solanio refers to him as Antonio's 'most noble kinsman' and Lorenzo addresses him as 'My Lord Bassanio'. His first words 'Good signiors both when shall we laugh? say, when?' reveal authority, friendliness of manner, control and the desire to be happy. In Act II, Scene 2 we see him clearly at ease when giving commands. Nerissa is most impressed by him when he first arrives in Belmont. The astute Portia is proud to be his wife. Gratiano has to go with him to Belmont, and Antonio 'only loves the world for him'. Indeed Antonio allows himself to fall deeply in debt and almost to sacrifice his life in order to satisfy Bassanio's wishes. So Bassanio inherently is a person who creates deep friendships, love and loyalty. He is the most favoured of Antonio's friends and the most favoured of Portia's suitors. Even the unpredictable Launcelot Gobbo is happy in his service.

The strength of attachments associated with Bassanio illustrate the themes of friendship, affection, and loyalty at work in the play. These qualities seem to transcend rank or financial position. At the beginning, when asking Antonio for a loan, Bassanio is frank with him and does not take advantage of Antonio's feelings for him. He does not disguise the fact that he is in debt: ''Tis not unknown to you Antonio/How much I have disabled mine estate.' Neither does he attempt to deceive Portia about Antonio's lost fortune in financing Bassanio's Belmont venture. Also in Act III, Scene 2 he tells Portia that all he has are intrinsic virtues:

'I freely told you all the wealth I had
Ran in my veins, – I was a gentleman, –
And then I told you true.'

Bassanio is a shrewd judge of character and urges Antonio not to accept Shylock's terms. He tells his friend 'I like not fair terms, and a villain's mind' (I,3). Although prompted by Portia, his reflections upon the appearance and reality theme prior to his choosing the correct casket – 'The world is still deceiv'd with ornaments' – reveal a philosophical element in his nature. His generosity of spirit emerges when he returns to Venice on his wedding day in order to assist Antonio in his hour of need. In an exaggerated manner he offers, during the trial scene, to sacrifice his wife for his friend. He keeps his word to Antonio and conceals the latter's part in the ring episode.

Bassanio has weaknesses. His slightly superior attitude to Shylock is not without its element of prejudice. He invites Shylock to dinner and unthinkingly ignores Shylock's dietary needs. His weaknesses initiate the action of the play. Bassanio has squandered his inheritance, he needs to borrow money in order to settle past debts as well as build up new ones. His motives in wishing to marry Portia are questionable. He confesses to Antonio to whom 'I owe the most in money and love' that he has 'plots and purposes/How to get clear of all the debts I owe'. Portia is crucial to these schemes. The first words he speaks about her – 'In Belmont is a lady richly left/And she is fair, and (fairer than that word)' – relate financial gain to physical attractiveness. Bassanio wishes to marry Portia for her money. Portia seems to accept the situation. She is not averse from irony at Bassanio's expense when he is ready, during the trial scene, to offer Shylock his wife's money.

Throughout the play Bassanio's language reflects the interrelationship between financial wealth and spiritual value. He dwells upon the words 'rich', and 'fair'. His speeches in the opening scene of the play draw attention to the prevalent biblical and classical allusions in *The Merchant of Venice*. His advice to Antonio 'To shoot another arrow that self way/Which you did shoot the first' alludes to the story in 1 Samuel, 20 18–22,35–40 in which Jonathan shoots arrows to warn David. In the first scene Bassanio reminds Antonio of the distinguished ancestry connected with the name 'Portia', and of the classical quests in search of both riches and love.

Bassanio is a contradiction. His motives are honest but questionable, and his actions nearly cost the life of his best friend. He is prepared to spend large sums of money and run up debts when neither the money nor the credit is his. He is generous, loyal and honest in personal relationships. Bassanio is meant to have inherited virtue. His very being exudes trust, stability and loyalty. In fact his presence commands credit. He contrasts with Shylock, whose very presence evokes hostility and prejudice. Perhaps Shakespeare, in indicating Bassanio's contradiction, wishes to make a point about how we judge other human beings. Bassanio is judged on appearances. He reflects before choosing the right casket that 'The world is still deceiv'd with ornament'. Bassanio still charms audiences.

Gratiano

... speaks an infinite deal of nothing (more than any man in all Venice)

In Bassanio's view Gratiano is 'too wild, too rude, and bold of voice' for Belmont. He tells him:

To allay with some cold drops of modesty
Thy skipping spirit, lest through thy wild behaviour
I be misconst'red in the place I go to,
And lose my hopes. (II,2)

Gratiano is Bassanio's foil. Gratiano's pairing with the vivacious Nerissa provides a dramatic contrast to Bassanio's winning of the 'gentle' Portia.

On his first appearance in the play Gratiano deliberately plays 'the fool' in a misguided attempt to cheer up Antonio. The play-acting element remains with Gratiano and the metaphor of performance, and putting 'on a sober habit' (I,2), stays with him. Gratiano's intentions are good, but his perception of the complexity of human emotions and feelings lacks sophistication. He has enough common sense during the casket scenes to say little.

Gratiano is content to play the role of amusing, talkative jester. His language is descriptive, idiomatic, perceptive, and at times downright bawdy. The last lines illustrate his frequent recourse to sexual jest and innuendo. His genuine love for Nerissa is evident during the trial scene in a line such as 'I have a wife, who I protest I love.' A somewhat unprincipled but native intelligence is displayed when in the last act Gratiano deflects possible trouble from Nerissa by blaming Bassanio for initiating the transfer of rings. The less attractive sides of his wit also emerge in the trial scene. Shylock is a 'damn'd, inexecrable dog!' He doesn't waste a moment to throw Shylock's own words back at him, taunting him, 'O learned judge! – mark Jew, a learned judge', and indulging in nerve-jangling repetitions at Shylock's expense: 'A Daniel still say I, a second Daniel! –/I thank thee Jew for teaching me that word.'

Gratiano is part of the Portia-Bassanio, Gratiano-Nerissa pairing. Gratiano's coarse humour illuminates and punctures the often sombre, Venetian-Antonio-melancholic orientated scenes. His continual harping on play-acting and sexual innuendo pin-point two important areas of concern in *The Merchant of Venice*: appearance and reality and the gratification of desires. After all, if Bassanio had not asked Antonio for money in order to court Portia, and Antonio with his wealth dispersed was forced to take a loan from Shylock, there would have been no *Merchant of Venice*. In this sense Gratiano's language and actions provide some kind of commentary upon the central actions of the play – a drama about desires and their gratification.

Lorenzo

How sweet the moonlight sleeps upon this bank!
Here will we sit, and let the sounds of music
Creep in our ears – soft stillness and the night
Become the touches of sweet harmony

Lorenzo, one of the Bassanio circle, is described in the *dramatis personae* as 'in love with Jessica'. He is a romantic, artistic, very fond of music and is given some magnificent poetry – especially in the last act. Lorenzo idealizes Jessica, whom he regards as 'wise, fair, and true/She shall be placed in my constant soul' (II,6). The impractical Lorenzo leaves the planning of their elopement to Jessica. He is a spendthrift – 'an unthrift love' – also confessing in the final act that Shylock's fortune comes to Jessica and he as 'manna in the way/Of starved people'. Clearly Lorenzo is charming. Portia regards him highly and commits 'into [his] hands/The husbandry and manage of [her] house' (III,4). There are negative sides to him. He puns continually on the word 'gentle' when describing Jessica ('gentle' and 'gentile' are easily confused, especially when heard). He attacks her father as 'a faithless Jew' (II,4), and has no scruples about eloping with Jessica without parental approval. Lorenzo has little or no conscience about the dishonesty and betrayal involved in Jessica's thievery. He feels he is doing Jessica a good deed by assisting her conversion to Christianity.

Lorenzo dramatically serves various functions. In the first scene his assignations with Bassanio (lines 69–70) add an element of intrigue and mystery to the plotting. He and Jessica are a link between Venice and Belmont. Lorenzo's attitude towards Shylock and his consciousness of Jessica's heritage adds to the atmosphere of anti-Jewish hostility evident in the drama. The highly-charged sexual nature of his relationship with Jessica contrasts with the relationship between Bassanio and Portia. In Act V his lengthy poetic lines are counterpointed by Jessica's staccato speeches. Their dialogue serves a dramatic function in allowing Portia and Nerissa time to arrive home and to remove their disguises. Similarly, in Act III, Scene 5 Lorenzo's and Jessica's banter gives Portia and Nerissa the opportunity to disguise themselves.

Lorenzo's and Jessica's witty cross-talk at the opening of the last act is full of sexual innuendo. Lorenzo's elaborate classical references to, for instance 'Trojan walls', 'Grecian tents', and 'Cressid', do serve to place their love in a universal context. Lorenzo is given lines celebrating the inner musical harmony of the universe and eternal values of romantic love where 'Such harmony is in immortal souls.' Such harmony provides contrast to 'this muddy vesture of decay' – the harsh realities of the world depicted, for instance, in the Venetian scenes of *The Merchant of Venice*.

Jessica

Alack! what heinous crime is it in me
To be ashamed to be my father's child!

For a character making a relatively late appearance Jessica has an important structural role. She links Shylock's world with that of Venice and Venice with Belmont. Her name has Biblical origins. In Genesis, 11,26 'Abram and Nahor took them wives: the name of Abram's wife was Sarai; and the name of Nahor's wife, Milcah, the daughter of Haran, the father of Milcah, and the father of Iscah', i.e. Jessica who, according to some traditions, acted as a spy or look out. Certainly in *The Merchant of Venice* Jessica enters into a world alien from that of her upbringing in the Venetian ghetto.

A problem in interpreting the character and actions of Jessica is reconciling what the infatuated Lorenzo says of her with how she actually behaves. For Lorenzo Jessica is 'Wise, fair, and true' (II,7). But Jessica is deceitful, extravagant, disloyal to her father and her heritage, and a thief. Most of her actions generate from her hatred of her father and her love of Lorenzo. On one of the few occasions in which she reveals an awareness of her crimes she confesses 'Alack! What heinous crime is it in me/To be ashamed to be my father's child!' (Act II, Scene 3). Her hatred of Shylock is intense: 'But though I am a daughter to his blood/I am not to his manners.' Indeed she is extravagant, spending 'fourscore ducats at a sitting' (Act III, Scene 1) and exchanges a turquoise ring for a monkey. She betrays her father, steals from him, gives up her religion and speaks against her father when she has safely arrived in Belmont.

Few reasons for the intensity of Jessica's hatred of her father are given except that she is bored at home, feels a prisoner and is pathologically opposed to Shylock. Jessica initiates the elopement. Lorenzo leaves all the planning to her. Portia doesn't hesitate to leave her as mistress of Belmont. Jessica adapts well to her new surroundings. She reveals an astute awareness of prevailing power structures by remaining almost mute whenever Portia is present. Jessica's witty poetic dialogue with Lorenzo at the begining of Act V reveals that she is educated and certainly can trade classical allusions with him. Perhaps her final words in the play, 'I am never merry when I hear sweet music' indicate a sad, long-term future for her, and one far removed from the familiar family surroundings she has so willingly shaken off.

It is possible to excuse her behaviour in her own words. After heedlessly throwing a valuable casket to Lorenzo, a casket which doesn't belong to her, she notes that 'love is blind, and lovers cannot see/The pretty follies that themselves commit.' The immediate context of the speech reveals that Jessica is more embarrassed at being 'transformed to a boy' (Act II, Scene 6) than robbing her father.

She is first encountered in the play expressing sympathy for Launcelot Gobbo who is about to leave her father's service. She uses Launcelot to convey a message to Lorenzo – an illustration of the scheming she practises in order to elope with Lorenzo. Launcelot has a genuine affection for her. Lorenzo refers to her as his 'torch-bearer' and as 'issue to a faithless Jew'. She believes that her love for Lorenzo and conversion can 'end this strife', and be a bridge between two opposed worlds. There is some irony then in the fact that Jessica's encounters with Launcelot and Lorenzo contain the expression of religious prejudice directed not at her but at her father. In Act III, Scene 5 Launcelot's references to pork and other innuendoes become unpleasant. In short then, Jessica dramatically has an important function in bridging various worlds of the play and in thematically representing some of the fundamental issues at the heart of *The Merchant of Venice*: loyalty, fidelity, love, religion.

Nerissa

that same scrubbed boy (the doctor's clerk)

In Italian 'Nerissa' means small and dark. She serves Portia faithfully, acts as her messenger, during the casket scene, reminds Portia of Bassanio (see Act II, Scene 9), and helps to bring them together. Vivacious, she is close to her mistress, who discusses private affairs with her, and implicitly trusts her. Gratiano, when marrying Nerissa, does not feel that he is marrying beneath him, and her lack of subservience to Portia suggests that she is from a respectable background. Nerissa's sense of humour and intelligence are illustrated on several occasions; she quibbles on the word 'stake' with Gratiano (III,2), and enjoys puns and colloquialisms, throwing Gratiano's words about 'a little scrubbed boy' back at him – she is 'that same scrubbed boy (the doctor's clerk)' (V, 1). Argumentative, and provoking argument, her longest speech (see Act V, Scene 1) is directed at Gratiano. She enjoys role-playing, she has been disguised as a 'judge's clerk', and practised deception, yet the speech (lines 151–158) reveals her preoccupation with fidelity and trust in human relationships. The word 'ring', not lacking in sexual innuendo is associated with her. Its other reverberations of, for instance, attachment, honour, and connection, directly relate to her role in the play.

Nerissa is a foil to Portia as Gratiano is to Bassanio. Physically and mentally, in terms of stage presence, she balances the Portia-Bassanio-Gratiano relationship. Nerissa is an illustration of *The Merchant of Venice*'s motifs of friendship and companionship, appearance and reality, trust and deceit. Unlike Antonio and Shylock, she will not be forsaken.

Salerio and Solanio

We'll make our leisure to attend on yours.

These classic hangers-on are often neglected in discussions of *The Merchant of Venice*. They are given some remarkably good lines, full of interesting imagery and language, and have a not unimportant dramatic function in the drama. In the opening scene, whilst trying to cheer up the melancholic Antonio, their language indicates many of the themes reverberating in the play.

Solanio's reference to the 'two headed Janus' suggests the element of role-play and performance. Salerio's depiction of Antonio's 'mind ... tossing on the ocean' suggests the close inter-relationship between psychological and material states of being. Literally, Antonio's wealth is bobbing up and down with the ocean waves. His thoughts are with his ships. Further, the idea of 'tossing' introduces a hint of sexual deviancy never quite removed from Antonio's presence in the drama.

In Act II, Scene 4 they play a minor role in explaining to the audience part of the deception played upon Shylock in order to smuggle Jessica away. They prepare for the masque. At the start of Act II, Scene 6 Salerio quips with Gratiano about 'Venus's pigeons' – the classical reference places Jessica's and Lorenzo's actions in perspective – they are not the first or the last eloping lovers. In the same scene Salerio's use of phrases such as 'love's bond' and 'obliged faith' place emphasis upon key words in the play when least expected. He lends a receptive ear to Gratiano's 'strumpet wind' speech – Salerio is very aware of the hazards implicit in trade which relies upon the sea and the weather.

Salerio's and Solanio's roles as commentators on Shylock's reactions to his daughter's elopement, and their observations that a Venetian ship has run aground, emerge clearly in Act II, Scene 8. As observers they can be more objective than the deranged Shylock, and they serve an important function in the play, that of giving the audience information. They provide reportage on others' actions and they comment on other characters' actions. Thus, for instance, it is Solanio who notes that Antonio 'only loves the world for' Bassanio. At the start of Act III they function as purveyors of gossip and of a kind of racial animosity which provokes Shylock into his plea 'Hath not a Jew eyes?'. Salerio appears in Belmont and bridges the two worlds of the play when he acts in Act III, Scene 2 as a messenger from Antonio bringing a letter announcing the loss of his ships and wealth. Salerio also informs the Belmont set what has taken place in Venice, and of how 'none can drive' Shylock 'from the envious plea/Of forfeiture, of justice, and his bond.' In the next scene Solanio acts as Antonio's comforter when he is imprisoned. Both are present at the trial scene, and Salerio announces the arrival of the disguised Portia.

The two have then a choric role. Dramatically they fulfil a

function in opening the play and presenting the apposite tone of trade, gambling, role-playing, and chance. Without them we would not learn about Shylock's reactions to his daughter's elopement, or the depth of Antonio's feelings for Bassanio. Salerio, in his role of letter-bringer from Antonio to Belmont, helps to create the trial scene, for it is he who informs Bassanio and Portia of Antonio's loss and imprisonment.

Launcelot Gobbo

The patch is kind enough, but a huge feeder

Launcelot appears in five scenes of the play, as servant, clown and messenger. His opening speech at the beginning of Act II, Scene 2 steers clear of colloquialisms, slang and dialect forms and uses instead learned words and literary expressions. The argument itself however is illogical. Launcelot begins by stating that though he has no conscience about running away, his conscience counsels against such a course of action. Subsequently in the scene he deceives his own father by pretending to be dead. He decides to leave Shylock's service because he is bored, meets Bassanio and enters his service. His appearances are characterized by ironic word-play and situational farce. His actions raise issues concerning conscience and the question of the loyalty of servants to their masters. His farewell to Jessica in Act II, Scene 3 exhibits genuine affection for her, and he begins his role of messenger, bridging the different worlds of the play. He takes a message to Lorenzo for her, and in the next scene takes one for Jessica from Lorenzo. He serves as a link between the world of Shylock and Jessica and that of Bassanio and Lorenzo. In Act II, Scene 5 we learn that Shylock is pleased to get rid of him for he is a 'snail', a 'drone', a 'wild cat', yet Shylock admits of Launcelot that 'the patch is kind enough'. Evident in this scene is Launcelot's intelligence and inventiveness, for he manages to get a message to Jessica and to play upon Shylock's superstitious nature. The riotous, uncontrolled elements in him emerge in Act III, Scene 5, when he challenges Lorenzo's control over Portia's household. Through dwelling upon Jessica's Jewishness, he introduces a note of sourness into the happy Belmont atmosphere. His verbal dexterity is evoked in images of food, legitimacy and illegitimacy. The final glimpse we have of him is in the final act when he is imitating the sound of the hunting-horn announcing Bassanio's return.

In short, Launcelot Gobbo is a wit, a clown, a messenger, and a linking device between the two main plots. He allows us to glimpse another side of Shylock – the domestic one. His switch of loyalties from one master to another echoes a theme in the play, that of loyalty and fidelity.

Style

This general heading can in no way encompass the variety of Shakespeare's usage in *The Merchant of Venice*, and accordingly the various sub-headings given below should be studied for their selective detail and references.

Prose and poetry

Prose is generally used by comic characters (e.g. Launcelot Gobbo), by characters of a lower social status (e.g. Gobbo and Nerissa), and for letters and formal modes of address (e.g. Bellario's letter to the court in Act IV, Scene 1). In *The Merchant of Venice* prose is used in the following instances:

1 In Act I, Scene 1, Gratiano's lengthy jesting speech to Antonio is followed by a few prosaic lines from Bassanio. The prose in its direct succinctness highlights Bassanio's comment that 'Gratiano speaks an infinite deal of nothing', although it is not itself devoid of imagery.

2 In Act I, Scene 2 prose is used when Portia speaks with her waiting-woman Nerissa.

3 In Act I, Scene 3 Bassanio and Shylock conduct their business discussion in prose. They return to poetry when Antonio enters.

4 In Act II, Scene 2 Launcelot Gobbo's opening speech and subsequent lines are in prose. Gobbo doesn't indulge in slang or dialect words, but he is a servant and has a comic role. His father, as a member of the lower classes and cast in the role of a buffoon, is given prose, whereas in the same scene Bassanio and Gratiano speak poetry.

5 In Act III, Scene 1 the merchants Solanio and Salerio communicate in a factual prose which sharply contrasts with the evocative metaphoric verse of the preceeding Belmont scene and the one which will follow (in which Bassanio chooses the correct casket). Shylock too in Act III, Scene 1 uses prose when conversing with his friend Tubal. Incensed by Salerio and by what has taken place, he is provoked into the great 'Hath not a Jew eyes' speech. Delivered in impassioned poetic prose the

speech is dominated by rhetorical questions, repetitive mono-syllables and a controlled balance in sentence lengths which together create a powerful cumulative effect.

6 In Act III, Scene 2 Antonio's letter to Bassanio about the loss of his ships is in prose.

7 In Act III, Scene 5 Jessica and her servant Launcelot converse in prose, as does Lorenzo. Only when Launcelot has gone is blank verse used.

8 Bellario's letter to the court (Act IV, Scene 1) is in prose.

Apart from the above, *The Merchant of Venice* is dominated by blank verse (iambic pentameter lines without rhyme), and rhyming couplets which frequently announce a departure from the stage or the close of a scene or act. These are used for elaborate, witty and often bawdy punning – a good example may be found in the final lines of the play. The cryptic messages within the caskets are in rhyming couplets directly underscoring the messages which they convey. Surprisingly in a play with many musical references, there is only one song (Act III, Scene 2). The song 'tell me where is fancy bred' serves several purposes: 'bred' and 'head' rhyme with 'lead' and it could be argued that Bassanio is pointed in the direction of the correct casket. The song also reinforces one of the themes of the play – true worth is not to be found on the surface, appearances can be misleading.

Puns

The play is full of puns (a play on words, words having at least two different meanings) reinforcing serious, comic and bawdy mean-ings. Obvious examples are with the words 'fair', 'good', 'worth' and 'dear', all referring to financial standing and to human endearment or affection. 'Rings' refers to the commitment between partners. Portia and Nerissa revel in taunting their husbands with the loss of their rings. The word also means possession and has sexual implications. To take one other example from a text reverberating in puns – in the first scene Salerio tells Antonio that his 'mind is tossing on the ocean'. The word 'tossing' is an evocative pun. It can refer to Antonio's psychological state – his thoughts are restless: and it can refer to his material financial state – his wealth is bobbing up and down on the ocean in wooden hulks.

Set speeches

There are sustained set speeches in *The Merchant of Venice*: Portia's court-room comments about mercy, Shylock's rhetoric, Act V's opening romanticism focussing upon moonlight and the music of the spheres. We have yet another example in Bassanio's casket choice speech (Act III, Scene 2) which ranges in reference from dying swans (symbols of longevity) to classical exploits of love and heroism enacted during the Trojan wars.

Imagery

The play is full of evocative poetic images: for instance, Antonio's description of mountain pines 'fretten with the gusts of heaven' (Act IV, Scene 1), Gratiano's image of the 'scarfed bark' – a ship leaving a bay to be 'Hugged and embraced by the strumpet wind' (with its delightful personification of the wind as a prostitute, Act II, Scene 6), and the description in Act V of the 'floor of heaven' as a mosaic 'thick inlaid with patens of bright gold'.

Bassanio who thinks that Gratiano 'speaks an infinite deal of nothing' (I,1,114) pours out images. Particularly noticeable are those used when he chooses Portia in the casket scene and in the moonlit Belmont setting of Act V. However, images are well distributed amongst the characters and scenes. For instance in Act II, Scene 7 the Prince of Morocco describes Venice as a 'watery kingdom, whose ambitious head/Spets in the face of heaven.' Portia's suitors are described as coming 'o'er a brook' to see her, and Portia herself is punningly described as 'never so rich a gem/Was set in worse than gold' – a 'gem' being both a precious stone and Portia herself. In Act II, Scene 9 another suitor, the Prince of Arragon, uses the 'martlet' image to refer to the casket situation. The reference is particularly apposite, as martlets build nests in places which appear to be safe but aren't. In fact the 'martlet' reference really works against Arragon, for he too will be misled by appearances. After he has made the incorrect choice Portia, not without an element of relief, parallels his situation to that of a moth which had flown too close to the flame 'Thus hath the candle sing'd the moth.' Bassanio arrives to try his luck at choosing the correct casket soon after Arragon's departure. The contrast between the two and Portia's attitude towards the two is effectively made when Bassanio's messenger observes that 'A day in April never came so sweet.' The seasonal reference sets the tone for the imagery in Act III, Scene 2, in which Bassanio makes the right casket choice. The scene is full of images of fertility, pleasure and joy, ranging from 'the buzzing pleased multitude' of a crowd listening to a 'beloved prince' to the 'crisped snaky golden locks' which both entice and deceive.

Imagery in *The Merchant of Venice* is not confined to Belmont. Reverberating through the play are images of the sea, shipping, fortune, wealth, gold, romance, credit, security and insecurity (financial and psychological). These images, and others such as rings referring to actual physical rings, and to connections between people, to entrapment and imprisonment, serve to unify the various plot strands in the play. Portia loses her ring after the trial scene. She regains it on her return to Belmont. Antonio's loss of financial credit, the result of the loss of his wealth at sea, and his taking a loan from Shylock, are a consequence of his generosity to Bassanio so that Bassanio can pay court to Portia. It later emerges that Antonio's ships with their rich cargoes have not been lost at sea. The play opens with images of the sea surrounding Venice, it closes with the word 'ring'.

Imagery provides contrasts between scenes, moods and characters. It also points to many of the leading *motifs* of the play, such as the friendship between people represented by the exchange of rings, or the loaning of money, or the fidelity between people represented by the retention of rings given them by others or, in the case of Bassanio and Gratiano, the giving away of rings. Other *motifs* range from gambling, represented by the casket choice and trade on the perilous high seas, to appearance and reality. Portia and Nerissa dress up as lawyers, the caskets tempt and destroy suitors who choose incorrectly. Personal value and financial value are shown in the play to be very different things. Indeed imagery serves as a structural device, unifying the various plots and the contrasting settings.

Classical and biblical references

Bassanio, Portia, Morocco, Lorenzo and Jessica, not forgetting
Launcelot Gobbo, allude to classical myths and fables. Solanio's
reference in the first scene to the 'two headed Janus' serves to
illustrate the way such allusions function in the play. Janus the
Roman God had two faces, a happy one and a frowning one.
These twin faces reflect the appearance and reality theme in *The
Merchant of Venice*. Again, in the opening scene Bassanio men-
tions the story of the golden fleece – a richly prized trophy
sought after by many. His allusion anticipates his own subsequent pursuit of Portia – his golden fleece – at Belmont.

Biblical references are not confined to the Old Testament, and
range from echoes of passages in Galatians and Corinthians to
the Epistles to the Romans and Genesis. These references serve
two main functions:

1 They provide a commentary upon the action of the play
2 To indicate a moral, or moral meanings.

In Act I, Scene 3 Shylock's overt reference to a passage in
Genesis, 30,31–43, to Jacob, Laban and sheep transactions,
highlights traditional wisdom, fertility, productivity and stealth.
In Act II, Scene 6 Gratiano's reference to 'the prodigal' suggests
the story of the prodigal son wasting his allowance in luxurious
living with easy-going women and returning penniless to his
father. Gratiano's comment is made at the time Jessica is looting
her father's house and about to elope with Lorenzo. The
allusion is not without a touch of irony (the difference between
what is asserted and what actually takes place). Jessica isn't a
'prodigal' son but a 'prodigal' daughter bringing to Lorenzo – an
'unthrift' – what in fact becomes a lot of money.

Music

Music is present throughout *The Merchant of Venice* and domi-
nates the beginning of Act V which is set in Belmont. Here it
serves to emphasize the reconciling elements at work in the play:
the three sets of lovers are at last together, the financial problems are resolved, and even Gobbo the clown has found a home.
Music is also referred to in Act III, Scene 2 when Bassanio is
about to choose a casket and Portia orders music to be played. If

Bassanio chooses incorrectly 'he makes a swan-like end,/Fading in music.' If, however, he chooses correctly, trumpets flourish as 'To a new-crowned monarch', and 'dulcet sounds in break of day' will crowd upon him. The association of music with happiness and sadness is particularly noteworthy in the exchange between Lorenzo and Jessica as they await Portia's return at the beginning of Act V. Music evokes the inner harmony of the universe. It is also a means of judging others for, as Lorenzo tells Jessica:

The man that hath no music in himself,
Nor is not moved with concord of sweet sounds,
Is fit for treasons, stratagems, and spoils

In short 'Let no such man be trusted.'

Imagery, puns, exploitation of poetry and prose, biblical and classical references, are but a few instances of Shakespeare's brilliant use of many devices in *The Merchant of Venice* – a play in which most of the characters have certain specific images and ideas associated with them.

Further reading

The Arden Shakespeare: The Merchant of Venice, ed. J. R. Brown (Methuen).
The most scholarly text.

The Harmonies of The Merchant of Venice, L. Danson (Yale University
Press). A detailed account of the play.

Shylock on the Stage, T. Lelyveld (Routledge). The stage history of the
play.

The Stranger in Shakespeare, L. A. Fielder (Paladin Paperbacks).
Interesting on Shylock.

Shakespeare's Festive Comedy, C. L. Barber (Princeton University Press).
A standard book on comedy.

Pan study aids

Published jointly by Heinemann Educational Books and Pan Books

Pan Study Aids is a major new series developed to help school and college students prepare for examinations. All the authors are experienced teachers/examiners at O level, School Certificate and equivalent examinations and authors of textbooks used in schools and colleges worldwide

Each volume in the series:

- explains its subject and covers clearly and concisely and with excellent illustrations the essential points of the syllabus, drawing attention to common areas of difficulty and to areas which carry most marks in the exam

- gives guidance on how to plan revision, and prepare for the exam, outlining what examiners are looking for

- provides practice by including typical exam questions and exercises

Titles available: Physics, Chemistry, Maths, Human Biology, English Language, Geography 1 & 2, Economics, Commerce, Accounts and Book-keeping, British Government and Politics, History 1 & 2, Effective Study Skills, French, German, Spanish, Sociology

Pan study aids Titles published in the Brodie's Notes series

Edward Albee Who's Afraid of Virginia Woolf?

W. H. Auden Selected Poetry

Jane Austen Emma Mansfield Park Northanger Abbey Persuasion
Pride and Prejudice

Anthologies of Poetry Ten Twentieth Century Poets The Poet's Tale
The Metaphysical Poets

Samuel Beckett Waiting for Godot

Arnold Bennett The Old Wives' Tale

William Blake Songs of Innocence and Experience

Robert Bolt A Man for All Seasons

Harold Brighouse Hobson's Choice

Charlotte Brontë Jane Eyre

Emily Brontë Wuthering Heights

Bruce Chatwin On the Black Hill

Geoffrey Chaucer (parallel texts editions) The Franklin's Tale
The Knight's Tale The Miller's Tale The Nun's Priest's Tale
The Pardoner's Tale Prologue to the Canterbury Tales
The Wife of Bath's Tale

Richard Church Over the Bridge

John Clare Selected Poetry and Prose

Gerald Cole Gregory's Girl

Wilkie Collins The Woman in White

William Congreve The Way of the World

Joseph Conrad The Nigger of the Narcissus & Youth

Daniel Defoe Journal of a Plague Year

Shelagh Delaney A Taste of Honey

Charles Dickens Bleak House David Copperfield Dombey and Son
Great Expectations Hard Times Little Dorrit Oliver Twist
Our Mutual Friend A Tale of Two Cities

Gerald Durrell My Family and Other Animals

George Eliot Middlemarch The Mill on the Floss Silas Marner

T. S. Eliot Murder in the Cathedral Selected Poems

J. G. Farrell The Siege of Krishnapur

Henry Fielding Joseph Andrews

F. Scott Fitzgerald The Great Gatsby

E. M. Forster Howards End A Passage to India

E. Gaskell North and South

William Golding Lord of the Flies Rites of Passage The Spire

Oliver Goldsmith Two Plays of Goldsmith: She Stoops to Conquer;
The Good Natured Man

Graham Greene Brighton Rock The Human Factor
The Power and the Glory The Quiet American

Willis Hall The Long and the Short and the Tall

Thomas Hardy Chosen Poems of Thomas Hardy
Far from the Madding Crowd Jude the Obscure
The Mayor of Casterbridge Return of the Native
Tess of the d'Urbervilles The Trumpet-Major

L. P. Hartley The Go-Between The Shrimp and the Anemone

Joseph Heller Catch-22

Ernest Hemingway A Farewell to Arms

Susan Hill I'm the King of the Castle

Barry Hines Kes

Aldous Huxley Brave New World

Henry James Washington Square

Ben Jonson The Alchemist Volpone

James Joyce A Portrait of the Artist as a Young Man

John Keats Selected Poems and Letters of John Keats

D. H. Lawrence The Rainbow Selected Tales Sons and Lovers

Harper Lee To Kill a Mockingbird

Laurie Lee Cider with Rosie

Thomas Mann Death in Venice & Tonio Kröger

Christopher Marlowe Doctor Faustus Edward the Second

W. Somerset Maugham Of Human Bondage

Gavin Maxwell Ring of Bright Water

Arthur Miller The Crucible Death of a Salesman

John Milton A Choice of Milton's Verse Comus and Samson
Agonistes Paradise Lost I, II

Bill Naughton Spring and Port Wine

L. O'Brien Z for Zachariah

Sean O'Casey Juno and the Paycock
The Shadow of a Gunman and the Plough and the Stars

George Orwell Animal Farm 1984

John Osborne Luther

Alexander Pope Selected Poetry

Siegfried Sassoon Memoirs of a Fox-Hunting Man

Peter Shaffer The Royal Hunt of the Sun

William Shakespeare Antony and Cleopatra As You Like It
Coriolanus Hamlet Henry IV (Part I) Henry IV (Part II) Henry V
Julius Ceasar King Lear Richard III Love's Labour's Lost
Macbeth Measure for Measure The Merchant of Venice
A Midsummer Night's Dream Much Ado About Nothing Othello
Richard II Romeo and Juliet The Sonnets The Taming of the Shrew
The Tempest Twelfth Night The Winter's Tale

G. B. Shaw Pygmalion Saint Joan

Richard Sheridan Plays of Sheridan: The Rivals; The Critic;
The School for Scandal

John Steinbeck The Grapes of Wrath Of Mice and Men & The Pearl

Tom Stoppard Rosencrantz and Guildenstern are Dead

Jonathan Swift Gulliver's Travels

J. M. Synge The Playboy of the Western World

Dylan Thomas Under Milk Wood

Flora Thompson Lark Rise to Candleford

Anthony Trollope Barchester Towers

Mark Twain Huckleberry Finn

Keith Waterhouse Billy Liar

John Webster The White Devil

H. G. Wells The History of Mr Polly

Oscar Wilde The Importance of Being Earnest